BAKING

WITH

BRUNO

A FRENCH BAKER'S

NORTH AMERICAN

LOVE STORY

BAKING

═══ WITH ═══

BRUNO

A FRENCH BAKER'S

NORTH AMERICAN

LOVE STORY

CHEF Bruno Feldeisen

EDITED BY
Michele Marko

PHOTOGRAPHY BY
Henry M. Wu

whitecap

DESIGN Andrew Bagatella
EDITOR Michele Marko
PROOFREADER Holly Doll
PHOTOGRAPHY BY Henry M. Wu

Library and Archives Canada Cataloguing in Publication

Title: Baking with Bruno : a French baker's North American love story / Chef Bruno Feldeisen;
    edited by Michele Marko; photography by Henry M. Wu.
Names: Feldeisen, Bruno, author.
Description: Includes index.
Identifiers: Canadiana 20190223286 | ISBN 9781770503328 (softcover)
Subjects: LCSH: Cooking. | LCSH: International cooking. | LCSH: Cooking, Canadian. | LCSH:
    Cooking, American. | LCSH: Cooking, French. | LCGFT: Cookbooks.
Classification: LCC TX725.A1 F45 2020 | DDC 641.59—dc23

We acknowledge the financial support of the Government of Canada through the Canada Book Fund (CBF) for our publishing activities and the Province of British Columbia through the Book Publishing Tax Credit.

Nous reconnaissons l'appui financier du gouvernement du Canada et la province de la Colombie-Britannique par le Book Publishing Tax Credit.

7 6 5 4 3 2 1

To my son Sergio,

A bundle of joy appeared in my life more than 12 years ago. I would walk around the maternity ward holding you in my arms, softly singing to your delicate ears the French song "A la clairefontaine". I was mesmerized by how beautiful and meaningful my life has become from the moment I first saw you. And today I am in awe of how beautiful and inspiring you have become.

I dedicate this book to you. Don't stop dreaming of snowy days on the hills; destroy as many skateboards as needed. Don't hold back and live a meaningful life, full of joy and happiness.

Your Dad.

CONTENTS

FOREWORD

By Mia Stainsby

A blast of fiery heat transforms batter—an embryonic mess—into something completely different, something that gives pleasure and joy. That is the magic of baking.

It's like the story of pastry chef Bruno Feldeisen's life and livelihood. Raised by a drug-addicted mother, his childhood in France was a baptism of fire. And yet here he is, a celebrated pastry chef who believes in the sweet, healing power of baking, his stretchy smile broadcasting a happy place in life.

At 16, he endured the hard knocks of being a chocolatier's apprentice like his life depended on it. In retrospect, it did. It transformed him. I once interviewed him for a story for the *Vancouver Sun* and he shared how that apprenticeship was his salvation.

"I was part of a family . . . That kitchen helped me become a man. The kitchen is a little society. It's life. The table is designed to bring people together. There is something primal, emotional and raw about it. Kitchens became an escape for me and when I was younger, the chefs I worked for were like father figures."

His near-perfect score on his exam kickstarted his career at famous A-list restaurants around the world. He worked at Le Louis XV (Alain Ducasse) in Monaco, at Patina Restaurant in Los Angeles, and in the kitchens of Four Seasons hotels in the U.S. and Vancouver. He's been a pastry instructor, and now, a TV personality.

"Being in the kitchen and growing my career in North America was and still is my salvation," he says. "I fell in love with North America 30 years ago, was mesmerized by how people really enjoyed food without being snobs. The great open spaces of North America equates to great open minds for me," he says.

This first cookbook is aptly titled *Baking with Bruno: A French Baker's North American Love Story*. "They're recipes I collected over the past 30 years. North America has a strong baking history that came with its waves of immigrants," he says. There was a time when Bruno's past came to roost upon him, but he sought help and he took what he learned to help others and he's now a spokesperson for a mental health advocacy group, Anxiety B.C.

"The book is about a love story—moi and all the baking and desserts that have excited my mind for the past 30 years."

Maybe you'll find that magic, going on this baking journey with him. Most people bake in anticipation of sharing or giving, and the process itself is therapeutic. There's nothing like pulling out the mixer to soothe the soul.

For Bruno, this cookbook honours the kitchen and the craft that gave him a notable life, and he shares that "little society" that nurtured him as a 16-year-old.

HELLO! MY NAME IS BRUNO

This book of recipes documents my discovery of North American food culture in the context of my French culinary background. Going from a distinct old-world culture with very defined culinary rules to a land where anything seemed possible—especially for newcomers—made my exploration all the sweeter. This is my ode to that delightful journey.

HOW DID I GET THERE?

My first vivid memory of tasting something sweet is deeply interwoven with a sense of excitement and escape. I was about four years old and my mother and I were flying one evening from Clermont-Ferrand—our small hometown—to Paris. Back in the '60s, the airport terminal wasn't more than a wooden shack. We were flying on an Air Inter Nord 42 propeller plane. We walked across the tarmac with our suitcases to board the plane. I remember the strong smell of jet fuel and the flash of brilliant, clear blue lights of the runway. On board, the seats were plush, the kind you could sink into. Then the flight attendant appeared before me with a basket filled with sucettes—or in English, lollipops. She handed me the biggest lollipop I had ever seen—I mean a foot-long lollipop—a most delicious pretty thing that I devoured as we were departing. The whole plane shook with the roar of the engines and the force of speed as we gained altitude. It was my first memory of something sweet and exciting. From that I recall, almost as a sensation, a burst of freedom.

From this well entrenched sweet memory, I have developed two life passions: creating anything sweet, and a life-long love of planes. My dream as a child was to be a pilot. One passion became a successful career. The other one takes me to airport runways where I am still mesmerized by how gracious planes appear as they take off or land.

Never forgetting that planes are still vessels of dreams, in 1988, I embarked on a search of new horizons, open spaces and new flavours, and landed in New York. That is a journey I have never regretted— a North American love story where I have cooked alongside cooks from every walk of life in cities as vibrant as my curiosity. I discovered that food in North America was tasty, exciting, culturally rich and that the desserts were delicious. The first cookbook I bought after arriving was *An American Baker* by Chef Jim Dodge. I learned how entrenched baking was here, how centuries of immigrants from Holland, Germany, Italy and other distant places made this a land where I would learn and discover. I fell in love, and, 30 years later, I still get excited, learning new techniques and recipes.

Here are a few of my favourite recipes, from my heart to yours, to enjoy at home among family and friends. The kitchen is the heartbeat of the house; let the sweet smells of baking create long-lasting memories.

Bruno

CHEF BRUNO'S PANTRY

There is never enough shelf space in my kitchen. Every time I go shopping for food—either at my local grocery store or at a farmer's market—my eyes are always on alert to find a spice I have never heard of, a local farmer crafting artisan butter or a flour mill working ancient grains. I always choose local and ethical over organic; the welfare of animals and the livelihood of local farmers trump any politically correct labels.

Our North American backyard is richer than we think, with a long history of artisans, small family companies and farmers. But at the end of the day, only buy ingredients you love and feel comfortable baking with. You are the captain of your kitchen, and the world is a big garden, so never stop discovering. Be hungry for more delectable sweets and bakes.

The list below is only for reference.

BERRIES: always keep a few bags of different types of berries in your freezer. In summer, at the sight of colourful mountains of berries exhibited at farmers markets, I can never resist them and always buy more berries than needed, and stock my freezer with juicy and sweet berries for the winter months.

BUTTER: all my recipes use unsalted butter. The only salted butter I use is artisan made. I find industrial brands overly salted, therefore affecting the result of any baking.

CANNED FRUITS: peach and pineapple chunks come in so handy. Canned fruit helps you to create, at the spur of the moment, a great upside-down cake or fruit financier.

CHOCOLATE: any dark chocolate with a cocoa content of 64% and above is delicious. Everyone has their own favourite. For milk chocolate, brands with a cocoa solid of 34% and above are good. I never believed you need to spend a lot of money on expensive brands. Once you find a brand you love, stick with it.

COFFEE: instant coffee is so versatile and easy to use. In any recipe, 1 tsp. (5 mL) gives you a café latte flavour, but 4 tsp. (20 mL) translates into a strong espresso.

CORN KERNELS: there is nothing cheaper to store and more satisfying to pop than corn kernels, topped with some real melted butter and sea salt or simply drizzled with caramel.

DRIED FRUITS: apricots, cranberries, raisins, dates, figs. Just be aware that dried fruit can sometimes be overly dry because of faulty storage or just being too old. If buying in bulk, check the quality, and once home, store them in an airtight container.

EGGS: for consistency, every recipe in this book uses large eggs, always at room temperature.

FLOUR: most brands will do, but remember that all bleached flours are indeed whitened with a bleach chemical process. I am fine using them, but there are a lot of alternative organic flours to choose from at a higher price point.

GINGER: candied Australian ginger is a must. Soft and tender, not overly sweet.

HONEY: again choose locally-sourced products. Plenty of choice at any local farmers markets year round.

MAPLE SYRUP: be sure to use 100% pure maple syrup. A bit pricey, but definitely better that any "flavoured maple syrup" laced with corn syrup.

NUTS: pecans, walnuts, ground almonds. Keep them in airtight containers in a freezer to keep them fresh.

SEA SALT: plenty of varieties to choose from, with a few French and Italian brands easily available at any large grocery chain, at a very low price. No need for fancy sea salts from exotic places, often at exorbitant prices.

SPICES: cinnamon, nutmeg, coriander, cardamom, either ground or in its natural shape.

SUGAR: granulated, light brown, and icing are the three main sugars needed. A key point to remember, white sugar is not vegan. In most cases cane juice is passed through filters filled with crushed beef bones.

VANILLA: vanilla beans and 100% pure vanilla extract. Read the label when buying vanilla extract and stay away from artificial flavouring like vanillin, a synthetic chemically extracted from wood products.

TOOLS OF THE TRADE

I could write pages about what equipment is needed to be a baker, and my kitchen is a testament of how much one baker thinks he needs to acquire. But the truth is you don't need a lot to be a successful baker and you can build your baking tool inventory over time. Today, there are plenty of discount stores that sell kitchen and baking ware at reasonable prices. Here's my guide to helpful tools to have in your kitchen.

BLOWTORCH Best tool to caramelize the top of crème brûlée.

CANDY THERMOMETER They are also called sugar thermometers. I use a basic one like a Norpro brand.

CUTTERS Set of both straight and fluted ones.

ELECTRIC MIXER Always the most expensive piece of equipment. You could do without it for a while, but it is a challenge, at least for making cookies.

KNIVES Plenty of great knives at reasonable prices, unless of course you aspire to be a sushi Master. A small paring knife, bread knife and Chef's knife will do.

MADELEINE MOULD Get a Teflon-coated one.

MOULDS Cake moulds, different shapes and forms always enhance presentations and eye appeal. But a creative baker can always use an empty soup can or take a trip to a local hardware store to buy some metal pipes in any sizes you want.

PASTRY BRUSH With synthetic bristles which are easier to clean and sanitize.

PIPING BAGS Disposable in plastic are more sanitary.

PIPING TIPS An assorted set of different sizes.

ICE CREAM SCOOP Handy to portion and scoop cookies and muffins.

ROLLING PIN Always in wood, I mostly use the French style, but it is easier to use a rolling pin with handles.

SAUCEPANS Small, medium and large.

SCALE & MEASUREMENTS A digital scale, measuring spoons, liquid measuring cup and a set of dry measuring cups.

SHEET TRAYS A hallow rectangle sheet trays with a 1-inch (2.5-cm) lip on all four sides. Be sure they fit in your oven, fridge and freezer before buying them.

SMALL SIEVE To strain all the custards, curds and sauces.

SPATULA Small, medium and large, both straight and offset.

DEEP PANS At least one spring-form pan to cook cheesecake in.

ZESTER Microplane brand is the best.

WHISK Medium size, both rigid and balloon style, which are great to create a lot of aeration in a foam.

WOODEN SPOON Medium size. Best to stir jams and fruit sauces as they cook.

BAKING & KITCHEN GLOSSARY

We chefs often use coded language or technical terms that are rooted either in the Italian or French lexicon. Below are brief descriptions of the many baking and cooking terms you will encounter in this book. This should take away some of the fear of not understanding some of the recipe process. I also encourage the reader to just Google any term for more clarification.

AERATION: to incorporate air into a batter or fat component with a fast whisking process.

BAIN-MARIE: french word for a double boiler.

BLEND: mixing 2 substances together.

BROWN BUTTER: cooked butter that has boiled in a saucepan to turn into a light brown colour and to develop a nutty flavour.

COOLING: allows an ingredient or baked good to cool down at room temperature.

EGG WASH: beaten eggs, sometimes some water or milk added to it, to be brushed on the top of a dough before baking to create a beautiful and shiny glaze when baked.

EXTRACT: an enhanced, concentrated substance such as vanilla, lemon or almond. Always be sure they are 100% pure, free of chemical or artificial flavours.

FLUFFY: something light and delicate, usually with a process of aeration.

FOLDING: gently incorporating by hand two different mixes or batters using a rubber spatula. The action of folding has to be gentle to avoid depleting one or both of the batter characteristics like aeration.

PATE: this is the French word for dough.

PAR BAKING: baking technique in which the rolled and pan-lined dough is partially baked to about 70%. Usually the baked goods have no baking colouration.

SIEVE: a small mesh utensil used to remove any particles or lumps to achieve a desired smooth product.

SIMMERING: the process to bring a liquid over low heat right before its boiling point for a determined length of time to achieve a required texture or flavour enhancement.

SPRING BACK: when checking if a cake or sponge is cooked properly by gently pressing the top of the bake to see if it "springs back" once it has been pressed.

SPRINKLE: to dust any top or surface with another raw ingredient, usually before baking, to create a new texture, pattern or design.

WHISKING: creating aeration while whipping at high speed with a whisk, either by mechanical process or using a hand whisk.

ZEST: the outer skin surface of a citrus that has been removed or harvested with a rapping technique using a citrus zester or a Microplane zest tool.

The Fundamentals

CHAPTER 1

The Fundamentals

In this first chapter, I introduce some of the basics of baking and pastry recipes. These are the fundamentals needed to create a simple fruit tart or baked pie.

Once you have the basics mastered, you can get creative and play with them. Be your own magical baking wizard by putting together different components.

FOR EXAMPLE

Pasta Frola + Pastry Cream + Fresh Berries = Delicious Fresh Berry Tart

Very Chocolaty Chocolate Dough + Chocolate Frangelico Frangipane + Banana = Delicious Baked Tart

Meringue +Pastry Cream + Fresh Blueberries = Blueberry Pavlova

Pâte Sablée

{ TWO 8-INCH (20-CM) ROUND SHELL TARTS }

This is the classic French short-crust pastry dough that is used to create the shell for lemon or fruit tarts. Rich and flavourful, this is my favourite dough to use for fruit tarts.

INGREDIENTS

2 cups (500 mL) all purpose flour

1¼ (310 mL) cup unsalted butter

1 cup (250 mL) icing sugar

⅛ tsp. (1.25mL) sea salt

4 egg yolks

INSTRUCTIONS

Cut the butter into small cubes.

In an electric mixer, using the paddle attachment, cream together the flour and butter on low speed until it becomes a sandy texture. Scrape down the sides of the bowl using a rubber spatula. Add the sugar, salt and egg yolks. Mix on low speed until the dough mixture just comes together.

Empty the dough on a lightly-floured work surface. Work the dough with your hands just to fully incorporate the flour. Form the dough into a 2-inch (5-cm) thick flat rectangle brick and cover with plastic wrap.

Refrigerate for 4 hours before using.

TIPS & TWISTS

Add ½ tsp. of ground cinnamon to the icing sugar before mixing.

EQUIPMENT

Electric mixer. Rubber spatula.

Pasta Frolla Dough

{ ENOUGH FOR TWO 8-INCH (20-CM) ROUND TARTS }

*This is the typical Italian sweet dough that is very similar to the French pate
sucrée or sweet dough. Not as sweet as the other doughs, it can be used for savoury recipes.
It is not as sturdy and is more brittle than a basic sweet dough.*

INSTRUCTIONS In a bowl, combine together flour, semolina, sugar, sea salt, baking powder and lemon zest. Cut the butter into small cubes and rub into the flour mix until the mixture becomes sandy.

In a small bowl, whisk the eggs until slightly fluffy. Add to the flour mixture, and using your hands mix the dough together. Transfer onto a floured working surface, and finish mixing the dough until smooth. Shape into a small brick and wrap in plastic film.

Refrigerate for at least 12 hours.

The dough can be made weeks ahead and stored in the freezer.

TIPS & TWISTS ....
Add some ground cinnamon, or fresh ground coffee beans to taste, making this pasta frolla dough a bit more exciting.

EQUIPMENT ....
Large bowl. Small bowl. Small hand-whisk.

INGREDIENTS

3 cups (750 mL) all purpose flour

¼ cup (60 mL) semolina

½ cup (125 mL) granulated sugar

¼ tsp. (1.25 mL) sea salt

¾ cup (180 mL) unsalted butter

2 large eggs

1 tsp. (5 mL) lemon zest

Brown Butter or Beurre Noisette

{ MAKES 1½ CUPS (375 ML) }

The French translation is Hazelnut Butter, because as the butter starts to cook, it emanates a dreamy scent of hazelnut throughout the kitchen. I use brown butter to enhance flavours of any fruit pies. It has a rich aroma that makes any savoury or sweet dish stand out.

INGREDIENTS

3 cups (750 mL) unsalted butter

INSTRUCTIONS Melt the butter in a medium saucepan over low heat. As the butter starts to melt, it will start to foam, the water content will start to evaporate and the melting butter will change to a light golden colour. Browned milk parts will start dropping to the bottom of the saucepan. At this point, keep a close eye on it. After a minute or two, the colour will darken and an aroma of hazelnut will develop. Remove from the heat and allow to cool.

Pass through a fine mesh sieve to remove any burnt components.

Be careful not to pass the light brown colour stage or the butter will start to burn. If that happens, remove the saucepan immediately from the stove and place on the counter to cool down. Do not pour water in while it is still hot. Mixing water and hot oil is very dangerous.

TIPS & TWISTS

You can make your brown butter in advance and keep it refrigerated. It is delicious simply spread on toasted bread.

EQUIPMENT

Medium saucepan. Small sieve.

Vanilla Pastry Cream

{ MAKES 3 CUPS (750 ML) | ENOUGH FOR TWO 8–INCH (20CM) ROUND TARTS }

French pastries would never be so good without a good vanilla pastry cream.
It's the magical link between a crumbly and buttery tart shell, and juicy and sweet summer berries.
That velvety sweet tasty curd makes the whole pastry world feel better. Be careful. Just sampling
a spoonful of warm vanilla pastry cream can be highly addictive!

INSTRUCTIONS Using a small paring knife cut the vanilla bean in half lengthwise. Scrape the seeds into a bowl, together with the egg yolks, sugar and corn starch. Using a hand whisk, beat until the mixture turns pale yellow.

In a medium saucepan bring the milk to a quick boil. Pour over the egg mixture and stir well. Pour back into the saucepan and bring to a boil while consistently stirring with the hand whisk. Once it boils, remove from the stove and pass the pastry cream through a fine mesh sieve into a container. Cover the pastry cream with a plastic film, directly applied to the surface, to avoid creating any steam.

Refrigerate for 4 hours before using.

Pastry cream can be kept refrigerated for up to 5 days.

TIPS & TWISTS ....

There are an infinite amount of flavours that you can add to a pastry cream. My favourites are Kahlua, rum, coffee and cinnamon.

The vanilla bean can be substituted with ½ tbsp. (2.5 mL) of pure vanilla extract.

EQUIPMENT ....

Medium saucepan. Large bowl. Small bowl. Small hand-whisk. Small sieve.

INGREDIENTS

2 cups (500 mL) whole milk

6 large egg yolks

½ cup (125 mL) granulated sugar

4 tbsp. (60 mL) corn starch

1 vanilla bean

Extra Chocolaty Chocolate Dough

{ ENOUGH FOR TWO 8-INCH (20-CM) ROUND TARTS }

It is intimidating to make this dough. It tastes bitter and you never know when it is baked.
But its deep chocolate flavour creates a sharp contrast when used as a tart
shell for a fresh raspberry and lemon curd tart.

INGREDIENTS

1 cup (250 mL) unsalted
butter, diced

¾ cup (180 mL) icing sugar

1 egg yolk

1 large egg

½ tsp. (2.5 mL) sea salt

2 cups (500mL) all
purpose flour

5 tbsp. (75 mL) extra red
cocoa powder

INSTRUCTIONS

In an electric mixer, using the paddle attachment, cream together diced butter and icing sugar. Scrape down the sides of the bowl with a rubber spatula to ensure the mixture is smooth and free of butter lumps. Add the egg and egg yolk, mixing until well combined. Finally, add the flour, sea salt and cocoa powder.

Just mix enough, on low speed, until the dough comes together. Transfer onto a floured work surface, and finish mixing the dough until smooth. Shape into a small brick and wrap in plastic film.

Refrigerate for at least 12 hours.

Dough can be made weeks ahead and stored in a freezer.

TIPS & TWISTS

This is an amazing versatile dough. I use it for tart shells, but also for a simple chocolate sandwich cookie like an Oreo.

EQUIPMENT

Electric mixer. Large bowl. Rubber spatula.

Pâte Sucrée

{ ENOUGH FOR TWO TO THREE 8-INCH (20-CM) ROUND TARTS }

A sweeter dough with less flakiness than a traditional North American pie crust, it's perfect for making fruit tarts and even simple sugar cookies.

INSTRUCTIONS Cut the butter into small cubes. In an electric mixer on low speed, using the paddle attachment, cream the sugar and butter until smooth. Scrape down the sides of the bowl using a rubber spatula. Add the eggs one at a time to ensure they are well incorporated.

Add salt, lemon zest and flour.

Mix at low speed until the dough mixture comes together. Transfer the dough to a lightly floured work surface. Finish mixing the dough by hand. Form dough into a 1-inch (2.5-cm) thick brick and cover in plastic wrap.

Refrigerate for 4 hours before using.

TIPS & TWISTS ....
Add 2 tsp. (10 mL) of instant coffee to the sugar before mixing.

EQUIPMENT ....
Electric mixer. Rubber spatula. Zester.

INGREDIENTS

1 cup (250 mL) unsalted butter

1 cup (250 mL) granulated sugar

1 tsp. (5 mL) lemon zest

2 large eggs

3 cups (750 mL) all purpose flour

¼ tsp. (1 mL) sea salt

Simple Syrup

{ MAKES 1 QUART (1 L) }

Always have on hand some simple syrup. I use it to soak sponge, brush the tops
of baked loaves or to sweeten any fruit drinks.

INGREDIENTS

2 cups (500 mL) granulated
sugar

2 cups (500 mL) water

¼ cup (60 mL) light corn
syrup

INSTRUCTIONS Place all the ingredients in a saucepan. Whisk and bring
to a quick boil.

Remove from heat and let cool down.

Store in an airtight container in the refrigerator.

TIPS & TWISTS ....

Once your syrup is chilled, you can divide it and make different flavoured
syrups like lemon, coffee or cinnamon.

EQUIPMENT ....

Medium saucepan. Hand whisk.

Almond Cream

{ MAKES 1 QUART (1 L) }

This is the perfect filling for a baked fruit tart, particularly a French apple tart.
It can also be blended with an equal amount of vanilla pastry cream to make light soufflé-like baked pies.
For me, nothing is better than an out-of-the-oven baked fruit pie!

INSTRUCTIONS Using an electric mixer with a paddle attachment on low speed cream the butter and sugar. Scrape down the sides of the bowl with a rubber spatula to ensure the mixture is free of butter lumps. Mix at high speed for 1 minute to aerate the mixture. Add the eggs one at a time until they are fully incorporated, then add the vanilla extract.

In a medium bowl, stir the flour, corn starch, sea salt and almond meal together then add to the egg mixture and mix until all the ingredients are fully incorporated. Pour into a plastic container and keep refrigerated until needed.

TIPS & TWISTS ....

Add ¼ cup (60 mL) of rum to the recipe.

EQUIPMENT ....

Electric mixer. Medium bowl. Rubber spatula.

INGREDIENTS

1 cup (250 mL) unsalted butter

1 cup (250 mL) granulated sugar

3 large eggs

½ cup (125 mL) cake flour

2 tbsp. (30 mL) corn starch

1 tbsp. (15 mL) vanilla extract

1 cup (250 mL) almond meal

½ tsp. (2.5 mL) sea salt

Plain Buttercream

{ MAKES 1 QT. (1 L) }

This rich, buttery and oh-so creamy buttercream is so versatile. It works for any topping, filling or cake decoration.

INGREDIENTS

1 large egg

2 large egg yolks

½ cup (125 mL) water

1 cup (250 mL) granulated sugar

1½ (375 mL) cups unsalted butter, room temperature

INSTRUCTIONS Using the electric mixer with the whisk attachment, whip at high speed the egg and egg yolks for 2 minutes.

Place sugar and water into a saucepan over medium heat. Bring to a boil. Insert a sugar thermometer into the mixture and continue boiling until it reaches 220°F (105°C).

While still whipping the egg mixture, pour the cooked sugar, while still hot, down the side of the bowl. Whip for another 2 minutes until the mixture is light, pale and foamy.

Cut the butter into cubes and add to the mixture while still whipping. Continue to whip on high speed until the butter is fully incorporated and the buttercream is light. At this point you can flavour the buttercream as desired or as suggested in the Tips & Twists.

Store in an airtight container in the refrigerator up to 5 days.

Let the buttercream warm to room temperature for 2 hours before using.

TIPS & TWISTS ....

The recipe can be easily flavoured by adding, for example, lemon zest, instant coffee or ground cinnamon to create your favourite flavours.

EQUIPMENT ....

Electric mixer. Small saucepan. Plastic spatula. Sugar thermometer.

Chocolate Frangelico Frangipane

{ MAKES 1 QUART (1 L) }

An Italian twist on a French almond cream, this is a delicious
filling for a warm dessert.

INSTRUCTIONS Using an electric mixer, fitted with the paddle attachment, cream together butter and sugar on low speed. Scrape down the sides of the bowl with a rubber spatula to ensure the mixture is smooth. Mix on high speed for 1 minute to aerate the mixture. Add the eggs and egg yolk, one by one, until they are fully incorporated, and then add the vanilla extract.

In a medium bowl, stir together the flour, corn starch, cocoa powder, sea salt and almond meal and then add to the egg mixture, mixing until all the ingredients are fully combined. Finally, add the Frangelico and mix on low speed until completely incorporated.

Transfer to a plastic container and refrigerate until needed.

TIPS & TWISTS ....
Substitute the almond meal with finely ground hazelnuts and the Frangelico with 2 tsp. (10 mL) of pure almond extract.

EQUIPMENT ....
Electric mixer. Medium bowl. Rubber spatula.

INGREDIENTS

1 cup (250 mL) unsalted butter

1 cup (250 mL) granulated sugar

3 large eggs

1 egg yolk

½ cup (125 mL) all purpose flour

2 tbsp. (30 mL) corn starch

1 tbsp. (15 mL) vanilla extract

1 cup (250 mL) almond meal

6 tbsp. (90 mL) cocoa powder

¼ cup (60 mL) Frangelico

½ tsp. (2.5 mL) sea salt

French Meringue

{ MAKES 2 QTS (2 L) }

Crispy, light and melt in your mouth, this French meringue recipe is easy for beginners but versatile. Create delicate, crispy meringues, dipped in chocolate, or pipe it into a nest as a base for Pavlova.

INGREDIENTS

1 cup (250 ml) egg whites, at room temperature

½ cup (125 mL) icing sugar

¾ cup (180 mL) granulated sugar

1 tsp. (5 mL) vanilla extract

INSTRUCTIONS

Preheat the oven to 210°F (100°C).

Using an electric mixer with a whisk attachment beat the egg whites on medium speed. Once they start to foam, gradually add the granulated sugar, followed by the icing sugar. Once both sugars are incorporated, increase the mixer to high speed and beat until soft peaks form. Fold in the vanilla extract.

Transfer into a medium tip-fitted piping bag and pipe out the desired shape on a parchment-lined baking sheet. Place the baking sheet in the oven and bake for about 1 hour 20 minutes, or until the meringues are dry and crispy.

Time will vary on size and thickness of piped meringue.

Remove from oven and place on cooling rack.

Keep in an airtight container in a dry place.

TIPS & TWISTS ....

Be as crazy and wild as you want. Once your meringue is whipped, you can fold in any food colour, any nuts such as pecans or pistachio or any flavours like coconut, cinnamon or cocoa powder. Or as an example: pink colour, dry coconut and chopped pistachio. Fun and delicious.

EQUIPMENT ....

Electric mixer. Piping bag. Medium piping tips. Rubber spatula.

—— CHAPTER 2 ——

Jams, Sauces & Toppings

This chapter is full of delicious recipes good on their own or as an enhancement to any sweet you want to devour.

Blueberry Jam

{ MAKES 4 CUPS (1 L) }

Sweet and juicy blueberries: my favourite super food. When in season,
it is a lovely addition to any salad bowl but making jam is the metaphor of capturing memories
of summer. Homemade blueberry jam is a delicious staple for any pantry. This jam—
not too sweet but so flavourful—is easy to make.

INGREDIENTS

4 cups (1 L) fresh or frozen blueberries

2 cups (500 mL) granulated sugar

1 vanilla bean

2 tbsp. (30 mL) pectin + ¼ cup (60 mL) granulated sugar.

2 tbsp. (30 mL) lemon juice

1 tsp. (5 mL) fresh lemon zest

INSTRUCTIONS In a saucepan, combine the blueberries, sugar and lemon zest. Using a small paring knife, cut the vanilla bean in half lengthwise. Add the split vanilla bean to the blueberry mixture. Using a wooden spoon, stir gently and place on the stove over medium heat. Cook for about 12 minutes while stirring every minute or so.

In a small bowl, stir together the pectin and remaining sugar and sprinkle over the cooking blueberries while stirring, to avoid any pectin lumps. Add the lemon juice. Keep the mixture to a boil while constantly stirring. Cook for about 2 minutes after it boils.

Remove from stove and let cool for 15 minutes. Remove the vanilla bean. Transfer to a storage container and refrigerate.

TIPS & TWISTS ....

A delicious jam on its own but also excellent for topping a cheesecake or as a pie filling. In season, you can substitute blueberries for the amazing Saskatoon berries.

EQUIPMENT ....

Zester. Medium saucepan. Wooden spoon.

Butterscotch Sauce

{ MAKES 1½ CUPS (375 ML) }

The first time I heard about butterscotch sauce I got so excited as I believed it was made
of scotch and butter. Much to my disappointment, I learned otherwise. But nevertheless, it is a lovely
treat to enjoy, and a favourite indulgence is drizzling it on cheesecake.

INSTRUCTIONS Using a paring knife, cut the vanilla bean in half lengthwise. In a saucepan on medium heat, combine water and sugar stirring gently and bring to a boil. Let it boil until the sugar becomes a light-coloured caramel.

Remove from heat, and whisk in the cream. Don't lean over the saucepan as the steam emanating from it can burn. Add the butter, vanilla bean and condensed milk and return the saucepan to the heat and bring it again to a quick boil. No need to scrape the seeds out of the vanilla bean. They will dissolve during the boiling process.

Remove from heat, add the sea salt, stir well and then pass the butterscotch sauce through a fine mesh sieve.

Transfer to Mason jars or plastic containers, and refrigerate.

TIPS & TWISTS ....
Stirring a little scotch in the recipe makes it real butterscotch!

EQUIPMENT ....
Medium saucepan. Pairing knife. Wooden spoon. Small hand whisk. Fine mesh sieve.

INGREDIENTS

1½ cups (375 mL) granulated sugar

¼ cup (60 mL) water

⅓ cup (80 mL) unsalted butter

¾ cup (180 mL) whipping cream

¼ cup (60 mL) condensed milk

1 vanilla bean

¼ tsp. (1.25 mL) sea salt

Brown Sugar Oats Streusel

{ TOPPING FOR ONE 8-INCH (20-CM) PIE OR CRISP }

The crunchy oats in this streusel recipe add a unique texture when used as a topping on any pie or crumble. It is also quite delicious on its own once baked.

INGREDIENTS

1 cup (250 mL) cake flour

¾ cup (180 mL) light brown sugar

½ cup (125 mL) rolled oats

¾ cup (180 mL) unsalted butter

1 tsp. (5 mL) sea salt

1 tsp. (5 mL) baking soda

1 tsp. (5 mL) ground cinnamon

1 tsp. (5 mL) vanilla extract

INSTRUCTIONS

Cut the butter into small cubes. Place all the dry ingredients in the electric mixer bowl.

Using the paddle attachment, mix on low speed for 1 minute. Add the vanilla extract.

Add the butter and mix on low speed until the butter is blended in to create a sandy texture.

Keep refrigerated in an airtight container until needed.

Streusel can be kept up to 5 weeks when refrigerated.

TIPS & TWISTS

Add 2 tbsp. (30 mL) of ground coffee to the mix right before adding the butter.

EQUIPMENT

Electric mixer. Rubber spatula.

Extra Chocolaty Chocolate Sauce

{ MAKES 2 CUPS (500 ML) }

A versatile recipe that can be used for dipping or drizzling on top of ice cream, fruits or cakes.
Also when packaged in Mason jars, it makes a great gift for the holidays.

INSTRUCTIONS In a medium saucepan, heat milk, condensed milk, corn syrup and honey to a boil. Remove from the stove. Whisk in the chopped chocolate, cocoa powder and sea salt. Stir until the chocolate is completely melted. Return the saucepan to the stove over low heat and continue to stir, bringing the chocolate sauce to a quick boil.

Remove from stove. Pass through a fine mesh sieve.

Store in an airtight container.

Can be kept up to 2 weeks in a refrigerator.

TIPS & TWISTS ....

Add 2 tsp. (10 mL) instant coffee.

EQUIPMENT ....

Medium saucepan. Hand whisk. Small sieve.

INGREDIENTS

1 cup (250 mL) finely chopped, extra-bitter chocolate

3 tbsp. (35 mL) cocoa powder

1 cup (250 mL) whole milk

1 cup (250 mL) condensed milk

2 tbsp. (30 mL) honey

¼ cup (60 mL) light corn syrup

¼ tsp. (1.25 mL) sea salt

Rhubarb Compote

{ MAKES 5 CUPS (1¼ L) }

*It is so sad that the fresh rhubarb season is so short. I use this recipe as a topping
on vanilla ice cream, or on cheesecake. It can also be used as a flavour boost when mixed into
an apple pie filling. Alternatively because rhubarb season is so short, just buy a huge amount
at your local farmers market and start making jam to your heart's content.*

INGREDIENTS

4 cups (1 L) fresh or frozen
rhubarb

2 cups (500 mL) granulated
sugar

½ cup (125 mL) water

½ cup (125 mL) light corn
syrup

½ cup (125 mL) honey

1 tsp. (5 mL) lemon zest

INSTRUCTIONS

Combine all the ingredients in a medium saucepan. Using a wooden spoon, stir gently and place on the stove over medium heat. Once the mixture is boiling, cook for about 12 minutes, while stirring every minute or so.

Remove from stove and let cool for 15 minutes.

Transfer to a storage container and refrigerate.

TIPS & TWISTS

When using fresh rhubarb, use a peeler to remove the outer skin layer. It is usually thick and fibrous. Add 2 tbsp. (30 mL) of grenadine syrup or a drop of red food colour to create more vibrant colour.

EQUIPMENT

Medium saucepan. Wooden spoon

Caramel Sea Salt Popcorn

{ MAKES 1 QT. (1 L) }

Homemade caramel popcorn with sea salt is one of my favourite snacks.
You can store it in Mason jars to give away as tasty gifts, or use as a topping for ice cream
or a garnish on a chocolate tart—as seen on page 131.

INSTRUCTIONS Preheat the oven to 240°F (115°C).

In a medium saucepan, bring brown sugar, water and corn syrup to a quick boil. Reduce heat to medium, while stirring with a wooden spoon. Continue cooking until the mixture starts to caramelize into a light brown colour. Whisk in the butter and baking soda and stir until completely dissolved. Keep warm so it stays liquid.

Place the fresh popcorn in a large bowl, then pour the melted caramel on top. Toss with a wooden spoon until all the popcorn is completely coated with caramel. Sprinkle sea salt. Spread over a parchment-lined baking sheet.

Place in the oven and bake for 30 minutes, stirring every 10 minutes with a wooden spoon. Remove from oven and place on a cooling rack to cool. Once cold break down any large lumps of popcorn.

Place in an airtight container and store in a dry room.

TIPS & TWISTS ....
Add 1 tsp. (5 mL) of Cayenne pepper or cinnamon for a little kick.

EQUIPMENT ....
Wooden spatula. Medium saucepan. Large bowl. Medium hand whisk.

INGREDIENTS

3 cups (750 mL) of freshly popped corn

¼ cup (60 mL) unsalted butter

½ cup (125 mL) light brown sugar

¼ cup (60 mL) water

¼ cup (60 mL) light corn syrup

⅛ tsp. (.5 mL) baking soda

⅛ tsp. (.5 mL) sea salt

Buckwheat Streusel

{ TOPPING FOR ONE 8-INCH (20-CM) PIE OR CRISP }

Buckwheat has a delicious nutty flavour that marries so well with lots
of baked fruits, like cherries or peaches.

INGREDIENTS

1 cup (250 mL) buckwheat flour

½ cup (125 mL) light brown sugar

½ cup (125 mL) unsalted butter

1 tsp. (5 mL) sea salt

1 tsp. (5 mL) baking soda

INSTRUCTIONS Cut the butter into small cubes. Place all the dry ingredients in an electric mixer bowl.

Using the paddle attachment, mix on low speed for 1 minute. Add the butter and mix on low speed until the butter blends into the mixture creating a sandy texture.

Refrigerate in an airtight container until needed.

Streusel can be kept up to 7 weeks if refrigerated.

TIPS & TWISTS ....

Add 1 tsp. (5 mL) of almond extract.

EQUIPMENT ....

Electric mixer.

Raspberry Jam

{ MAKES 1 QT. (1 L) }

Making jam creates the best memories of summers long gone.
Lingering aromas are, in my opinion, more than pictures, the true makers of nostalgia.
Every jar of jam captures that unique and special moment.

INSTRUCTIONS In a saucepan, combine the raspberries, sugar and lemon juice. Using a wooden spoon, stir gently and place on the stove over medium heat. Cook for about 12 minutes while stirring every minute or so.

In a small bowl, stir together the pectin and remaining sugar and sprinkle over the cooking raspberries while stirring, to avoid any pectin lumps. Keep the mixture to a boil while constantly stirring. Cook for about 2 minutes after it boils.

Remove from stove and let cool for 15 minutes.

Transfer to a storage container and refrigerate.

TIPS & TWISTS ....
The perfect filling for Linzer Torte or simply as a topping for your morning buttered toast.

EQUIPMENT ....
Medium saucepan. Wooden spoon.

INGREDIENTS

4 cups (1 L) fresh or frozen raspberries

2 cups (500 mL) granulated sugar

4 tbsp. (60 mL) pectin + ¼ cup (60 mL) granulated sugar.

Cookies & Pretty Sweets

Irish Shortbread

{ MAKES 60 COOKIES }

The original recipe came to me during my time at the Four Seasons Hotel in New York,
from my assistant Paul who hails from Ireland. I fell in love with it right away: for its ease to make, amazing buttery
flavour and delicate crumble. I also enjoy dunking this shortbread in the Very Lemony Lemon Curd.

INGREDIENTS

2¼ cups (625 mL) unsalted butter, room temperature

1½ cups (375 mL) granulated sugar

½ tsp. (2.5 mL) sea salt

1 cup (250 mL) semolina (or fine ground cornmeal)

1 tsp. (5 mL) freshly grated lemon zest

2 tsp. (10 mL) pure vanilla extract

4 cups (1 L) cake flour

¾ cup (180 mL) granulated sugar for the topping

INSTRUCTIONS Preheat oven to 350°F (175°C).

In an electric mixing bowl, using the paddle attachment, cream the sugar, sea salt, vanilla extract and butter on low speed. Scrape down the inside of the bowl from time to time to ensure the butter mixture is well combined, free of lumps.

In a separate bowl, stir together the cake flour, semolina and fresh grated lemon zest, then pour it all at once into the butter mixture. Mix slowly at low speed until the dough comes together. Avoid over-mixing.

Spread the shortbread over the entire surface of a parchment paper-lined baking sheet. Use a rolling pin to make sure the dough covers the entire surface of the baking sheet. Using a fork, poke holes on the entire surface of the dough.

Place the pan on the middle rack of the oven and bake for about 35 minutes, or until the top is done to a light, golden brown in colour. Remove the shortbread from the oven, and place on a cooling rack. While still warm, cut into 3-inch x 1-inch (7.6-cm x 2.54-cm) rectangles using a paring knife and a metal ruler. Rub evenly the remaining ¾ cup (180 mL) of sugar onto the top of the baked shortbread while still on the baking sheet. Let the baking sheet completely cool down.

Remove each shortbread piece from the baking tray using a small offset spatula and place them in an airtight container for storage.

TIPS & TWISTS ....
Add 1 tbsp. (15 mL) of fresh, chopped thyme to the shortbread mix and you will get an amazing sweet treat to pair with many cheeses.

EQUIPMENT ....
Electric mixer. Rolling pin. Fork. Zester. Metal ruler. Small offset spatula. 8-in. x 11-in. rectangle baking sheet

Sablé Breton

{ MAKES 2 DOZEN MEDIUM SIZE }

*The Brittany region of France is known to produce some of the best butter and sea salt
in the world, and there is no question that a high-ratio butter cookie is simply sumptuous. I believe
this is the best cookie the French are baking. Buttery and crumbly: its trademark is the
square-cross mark on the top, made with a fork.*

INSTRUCTIONS Preheat the oven to 360°F (180°C).

In an electric mixer bowl, using the paddle attachment, mix the egg yolks and sugar on medium speed until the mixture becomes a pale, yellow colour. Add the soft butter, little by little, and continue to mix to create a nice aeration. Use a rubber spatula to scrape the sides and bottom of the bowl to ensure the dough is smooth.

Stir the cake flour and baking soda together in another bowl. Reduce to low speed, add the flour and mix until combined.

Transfer the dough to a floured work surface and shape into a 1-inch (2.5-cm). thick rectangle. Wrap in plastic and refrigerate for 6 hours. Using a rolling pin, roll the dough to a thickness of ½-inch (1.25-cm). Cut into 2-inch rounds (5-cm) and place on a parchment-lined baking sheet.

Combine any dough scraps, roll out again and cut out shapes until all the dough is used. Using a fork, crisscross the top of each cookie to create a nice square pattern. Place the tray in the refrigerator and chill for 1 hour.

In a small bowl, whisk the egg. Using a pastry brush, apply egg-wash to the entire surface of each cookie. Sprinkle a small pinch of sea salt on each cookie.

Place the baking tray on the middle rack of the oven. Bake for 15 minutes, then rotate the tray 180 degrees and bake for another 10 minutes. You want the cookies to have a nice light golden ring on the outside, and a lighter colouring in the centre.

Because of the egg wash, the cookies brown faster, so keep a close watch.

TIPS & TWISTS ....
Add 1 tbsp. (15 mL) of crushed fennel or lavender seeds to the dough during the mixing process to create a sable Breton with a floral hint. For this particular cookie, I love using a large crystal sea salt.

EQUIPMENT ....
Electric mixer. Rolling pin. 2 small bowls. Docking rolling pin or fork. Set of round cookie cutters. 9-inch x 12-inch (23-cm x 30.5-cm) rectangle baking sheet. Pastry brush.

INGREDIENTS

4 large egg yolks

1 cup (250 mL) granulated sugar

1 tsp. (5 mL) pure vanilla extract

1 cup (250 mL) unsalted butter, soft, cut into small cubes

1½ cups (375 mL) cake flour

½ tsp. (2.5 mL) baking powder

1 whole large egg for egg wash

1 tbsp. (15 mL) sea salt

Candied Rose Petals

{ MAKES 2 DOZEN }

Fragile like crystals, thin and delicate, I use candied rose petals to decorate cakes, summery fruit tarts or packaged in Mason jars for unique gifts.

They are so simple to make but have big impact aesthetically.

INGREDIENTS

24 clean, fresh rose petals

1 cup (250 mL) granulated sugar

½ cup (125 mL) egg whites

INSTRUCTIONS

Prepare a parchment-lined baking sheet. Take one rose petal and gently brush the entire front and back surface with egg white. Toss in the sugar and cover both sides. Place on the tray. Repeat for the next 23 petals.

Place the tray in a dry and warm area and let air dry for 24 hours.

Remove each petal and delicately place in an airtight container.

TIPS & TWISTS ....

This makes a great cake or dessert decoration.

EQUIPMENT ....

1 pastry brush.

Espresso Langues de Chat

{ MAKES 2 DOZEN }

This light, crunchy, thin French cookie, shaped like a cat's tongue, can be enjoyed on its own or sandwiched with raspberry jam or chocolate ganache. Thin and delicate, yet it has a lovely crunch when you bite into it under the tooth.

INSTRUCTIONS Preheat the oven to 350°F (175°C).

Prepare 2 parchment-lined baking sheets. Cream butter and icing sugar together in an electric mixer bowl fitted with the paddle attachment. Mix until smooth. From time to time, scrape the sides and bottom of the bowl to ensure the batter is free of any lumps.

Stir the flour, ground coffee and salt together. Add the flour mix in 3 parts on low speed. Add little by little the egg whites until the cookie batter is smooth. Scoop the batter into a piping bag with a ½-inch (1.25-cm) round tip.

Pipe the cookie batter into long thin lines, 3-inches (7.6-cm) long, leaving 2-inch (5-cm) spaces between each piped line of batter. The cookies will spread while baking.

Refrigerate for 30 minutes.

Using a small sieve, dust icing sugar over each cookie then place on the middle rack in the oven.

Bake for about 10 minutes until the edge of the cookies is a light colour. Remove from oven and place the baking sheet on a cooling rack. Use an offset spatula to delicately remove the cookies from the tray.

TIPS & TWISTS ....

You can substitute the ground coffee with a dash of ground cinnamon or crushed candy canes sprinkled on the top of the cookies before baking— making this recipe a great treat for the holidays.

EQUIPMENT ....

Electric mixer. Plastic spatula. Small offset spatula. Piping bag fitted with a ½-inch round tip. Small sieve.

INGREDIENTS

½ cup (125 mL) unsalted butter

¾ cup (180 mL) icing sugar

1 cup (250 mL) all purpose flour

¼ cup (60. mL) egg whites

¼ tsp. (1.25 mL) sea salt

2 tbsp. (30 mL) ground coffee

Chocolate & Pistachio Snaps

{ MAKES 6 DOZEN }

Curved and dainty, these cookies are intensely chocolaty and crispy. And being so thin, you would never know they have any calories in them.

INGREDIENTS

½ cup (125 mL) unsalted butter

1 cup (250 mL) icing sugar

½ cup (125 mL) orange juice

¼ cup (60 mL) all purpose flour

5 tbsp. (75 mL) unsweetened cocoa powder

¼ cup (60mL) chopped pistachio

INSTRUCTIONS

Preheat the oven to 360°F (180°C).

Line a baking sheet with parchment paper.

Using an electric mixer, cream together butter and icing sugar using the paddle attachment. Slowly add the orange juice. Use the plastic spatula to scrape down the sides of the bowl.

In a small bowl, stir together flour and cocoa powder. Add the flour and cocoa to the butter mixture and mix on low speed until it is fully incorporated and smooth. Transfer the mixture to a bowl, cover with plastic wrap and refrigerate for 20 minutes.

Place 6 rounded teaspoons of cookie dough onto the baking sheet. Using the back of a wet teaspoon, flatten the cookies into a round shape, ½-inch thick (1.25-cm). Ensure there is plenty of room for snaps to expand while baking, as they will double in size. Sprinkle the top of each cookie with chopped pistachios.

Bake until the dough begins to bubble, approximately 10 minutes. Take out of the oven and let cool just enough so that the chocolate snaps can be lifted with a spatula without breaking and placed on a cooling rack.

Once cooled, place the cookies in an airtight container and store in a dark place.

TIPS & TWISTS ....

Add small diced candied ginger or just lightly sprinkle some instant coffee before baking.

EQUIPMENT ....

Electric mixer. Rolling pin. Small offset spatula. Rubber spatula.

Halva Pecan Biscotti

{ MAKES 6 DOZEN }

Another delightful discovery from my time in New York, the creamy, nutty halva makes this biscotti recipe a perfect pairing for dunking in an espresso. This is also an eggless biscotti recipe.

INSTRUCTIONS Preheat the oven to 360°F (180°C).

Prepare a parchment-lined baking sheet.

Cream the butter and sugar using the paddle attachment of the electric mixer. Mix until smooth. From time to time, scrape down the sides and bottom of the bowl to ensure the batter is lump-free.

In a small bowl, stir together flour, baking soda and salt. Add the halva, pecans and flour mix to the butter mixture. Mix on low speed until the dough just comes together.

Empty the dough on a slightly floured work surface, and finish mixing it by hand. Place on a baking tray, covered with plastic wrap and refrigerate for 20 minutes. Once the dough is chilled, divide into four equal balls, and roll each of them into a 1-inch (2.5-cm) thick log.

Place the logs on a baking tray with a 2-inch (5-cm) space between them. Using the palm of your hand flatten the logs ½-inch (1.25 cm) thick. Brush each log with egg wash, and sprinkle with a generous amount of sugar.

Bake for 20 minutes.

Once cooked, place on a cooling rack. Slice each log in an 45 degree angle, ½-inch (1.25-cm) thick and place on a tray on their sides.

Bake for another 5 minutes at the same temperature. Allow to cool by placing the baking tray on a cooling rack.

TIPS & TWISTS ....

Pecans can be substituted with any nuts

EQUIPMENT ....

Electric mixer. Small bowl. Plastic spatula. Slicing knife. Cutting board. Pastry brush.

INGREDIENTS

1 cup (250 mL) unsalted butter, at room temperature

¾ cup (180 mL) granulated sugar

3 cups (750 mL) cake flour

1 tsp. (5 mL) baking powder

1 tbsp. (15 mL) whole milk

1 cup (250 mL) chopped halva

¾ cup (60 mL) pecan pieces

¼ tsp. (.5 mL) sea salt

TOPPING

1 large egg, beaten

¾ cup (180 mL) sugar

Vanilla German Kipferl Cookies

{ MAKES 4 DOZEN MEDIUM COOKIES }

My cousins and I affectionately called our grandfather Pepe le Moko. We always baked together during so many holidays—making these delicious but sometimes challenging cookies. Those sweet memories still linger in my mind today. Buttery, sweet and nutty describe a perfect and addictive combination.

INGREDIENTS

1¾ cups (430 mL) unsalted butter

1 cup (250 mL) icing sugar

4 egg yolks

2 cups (500 mL) all purpose flour

¾ cup (180 mL) ground hazelnuts (or almonds)

1 tsp. (5mL) orange zest

¼ tsp. (1.25 mL) sea salt

COATING

1 cup (250 mL) granulated sugar

1 cup (250 mL) icing sugar

1 vanilla bean

½ cup (125 mL) warm melted butter

INSTRUCTIONS Preheat the oven to 350°F (175°C).

Using an electric mixer with the paddle attachment, cream the butter and icing sugar until smooth. Add the egg yolks one at a time and mix until smooth. Combine the flour, ground almonds, sea salt, orange zest, and then add to the egg mixture. Mix on low speed just until the dough comes together.

Roll the dough into logs. Slice logs into ¾-inch (2-cm) thick and shape each log into a small crescent. Place on a parchment-lined baking sheet.

Bake for about 15 minutes or until a light golden colour.

INSTRUCTIONS FOR COATING Cut the vanilla bean in half lengthwise and using a small knife, scrape out the seeds and stir into the granulated sugar. Once the cookies are baked, remove the tray from the oven and place on a cooling rack. While the cookies are still warm, brush each one with warm butter, and using a spatula, delicately place each cookie first into granulated sugar, then into icing sugar.

Place on a rack to cool down.

TIPS & TWISTS ....

This is a German recipe. No tips or twists allowed.

EQUIPMENT ....

Electric mixer. Zester. Offset spatula. Rubber spatula. Chef knife. Pastry brush.

Lady Bird's Lace Cookies

{MAKES 6 DOZEN }

*When doing research on the history of desserts in North America, I stumbled
across a stack of recipes from the White House, from the turbulent 1960s. This one is from the
time of President Lyndon B. Johnson's administration. His wife, the former First Lady. "Lady Bird"
Johnson noted that, "Lace cookies are served alone or with fresh peach ice cream at the ranch.
They're also perfect for that special tea or brunch."*

INSTRUCTIONS Preheat the oven to 325°F (160°C).

Cut the vanilla bean in half lengthwise, and using the small paring
knife, scrape the inside to remove the seeds. Add to the flour and stir well
using a hand whisk. Add the coconut.

In a small saucepan, mix corn syrup, butter and brown sugar and cook
over low heat just until it is all dissolved. Do not let it boil. Pour the butter
mixture into the dry ingredients and stir well using a wooden spatula.
Transfer the batter to an airtight container and refrigerate for 2 hours.

Line a baking sheet with parchment paper or a non-stick silicon pad.
Drop teaspoonful balls onto the tray, leaving 3-inches (7.6-cm) between
them, as they will spread and touch each other.

Bake for 11 minutes or until light golden brown, then transfer the
baking sheet to a cooling rack. Using a small offset spatula, remove each
lace cookie and place in an airtight container.

Store in a cool, dry place.

TIPS & TWISTS ....
This makes a great cake, or any dessert, decoration. It makes a great gift,
presented in a Mason jar, with a beautiful ribbon and small card.

EQUIPMENT ....
Small offset spatula. Small saucepan. Medium bowl. Wooden spatula.
Paring knife.

INGREDIENTS

2 cups (500 mL) all purpose
flour

1 cup (250 mL) fine
unsweetened shredded
coconut

½ cup (125 mL) light corn
syrup

½ cup (125 mL) light brown
sugar

½ cup (125 mL) unsalted
butter

1 vanilla bean

Peanut Butter, Milk Chocolate Cookies

{ MAKES 2 DOZEN LARGE COOKIES }

*Sweet and salty is not a combination that most French people enjoy. They
don't know what they are missing. Soft, salty and chewy, these cookies tend to disappear from
the cookie jar quite fast. You can always find the culprit: cookie crumbles on the lips,
and an air of satisfaction lingering on their face.*

INGREDIENTS

1 cup (250 mL) unsalted butter

1 cup (250 mL) granulated sugar

1 cup (250 mL) light brown sugar

3 large eggs

1½ cups (375 mL) smooth peanut butter

2 cups (500 mL) all purpose flour

1 tsp. (5 mL) baking soda

1 cup (250 mL) milk chocolate, chopped

¼ cup (60 mL) icing sugar

INSTRUCTIONS

Preheat the oven to 360°F (180°C). Prepare a parchment-lined baking sheet.

Using an electric mixer with the paddle attachment, cream together butter and both sugars. Use a rubber spatula to scrape down the sides of the bowl to ensure the mix is free of butter lumps. Add the peanut butter and mix for 1 minute on medium speed to aerate the dough. Lower the speed then add the eggs, one by one, again using the rubber spatula to scrape the sides of the bowl.

In a small bowl, stir together flour, baking soda and chopped chocolate. Add the dry ingredients to the butter and sugar and mix slowly until it is all incorporated. Remove the dough from the mixing bowl and place in medium bowl. Cover and refrigerate for 1 hour.

Scoop well-rounded balls of dough using an ice cream scoop and place 2-inches (5cm) apart on the baking tray. Flatten each cookie with the palm of your hand into ½-inch (1.25-cm) thick. Dip a fork into cold water and press down on the cookies to create a crisscross pattern. Sift icing sugar on the top of all the cookies.

Bake for 12 minutes. Rotate the tray around and bake for another 5 minutes until the outer edges of the cookies are slightly brown but the centre is a lighter colour and softer.

Remove the tray from oven and place on a cooling rack.

TIPS & TWISTS ....
Milk chocolate can be substituted for extra bitter or white chocolate.

EQUIPMENT ....
Electric mixer. Rubber spatula. Small mixing bowl. Medium mixing bowl. Medium size ice cream scoop. Small sieve. Fork.

Parmesan Rosemary Biscotti

{ MAKES 3 DOZEN }

I am always looking for new additions to my cheese board or charcuterie tray.
Crackers and toasted bread are boring. Bake this tasty and unique biscotti. It is
really simple to make the perfect savoury snack for every cheese lover.

INSTRUCTIONS Preheat the oven to 360°F (180°C).

In an electric mixing bowl, blend the flour, sea salt and baking powder on low speed using the paddle attachment. Add the diced cold butter and mix until the butter starts to break down into a sandy texture. Add the Parmesan and rosemary.

In a medium bowl, whisk the eggs for a minute, then add the olive oil and milk. Mix well until incorporated. Start the electric mixer on low speed, then slowly add the liquid and mix until the dough comes together. Do not over mix. Transfer the dough to a floured work surface, and finish mixing with your hands.

Transfer the dough to a bowl, cover with plastic wrap and refrigerate for 30 minutes.

Divide dough into 4 equal parts and roll into ½-inch (1.5-cm) logs. Place on a parchment-lined baking sheet, 2-inches (5-cm) apart and with the palm of your hand flatten into ¼-inch (1-cm) thick.

Beat the egg, and, using the pastry brush, apply egg-wash to the entire length of the logs. Sprinkle the logs with sea salt.

Bake at 360°F (180°C) for 20 minutes. Remove from oven and let cool.

Once the biscotti logs are cold, place them on a cutting board and using a serrated knife slice in diagonal ¾-cm. thick.

Place on baking tray again.

Bake for another 12 minutes. Remove from oven and place on a cooling rack.

TIPS & TWISTS ....
Enjoy with cheese, a bowl of soup or with charcuterie. Substitute Parmesan cheese with an aged cheddar and the rosemary with basil or thyme.

EQUIPMENT ....
Electric mixer. Medium bowl. Small bowl. Serrated knife. Small hand whisk. Pastry brush.

INGREDIENTS

3 cups (750 mL) all purpose flour

¼ tsp. (1.25 mL) sea salt

½ tbsp. (7.5 mL) baking powder

½ cup (125 mL) unsalted butter, diced, cold

2 tsp. (10 mL) dried rosemary

½ cup (125 mL) parmesan cheese, grated

2 large eggs

½ cup (125 mL) extra virgin olive oil

¼ cup (60 mL) homogenized milk

EGG WASH

1 egg

Pinch of sea salt

Lemon Honey Madeleines

{ MAKES 2 DOZEN MEDIUM SIZE }

A spongy cloud-like small cake, it was loved with devotion by French writer Marcel Proust.
Often novice bakers are intimidated by them, but they are really simple to make. A good tip is to let
the cake batter rest overnight, and, of course, to use a Madeleine baking tray.

INGREDIENTS

1 cup (250 mL) all purpose flour

¼ tsp. (1.25 mL) baking powder

⅛ tsp. (.5 ml) sea salt

2 large eggs

¼ cup (60 mL) honey

½ cup (125 mL) granulated sugar

1 tsp. (5 mL) fresh grated lemon zest

½ cup (125 mL) brown butter (see recipe page 18)

INSTRUCTIONS

Preheat the oven to 370°F (185°C).

In the electric mixer, using the whisk attachment, beat the eggs, sugar and honey on high speed for about 10 minutes until the mixture forms a golden, thick-ribbon texture.

Sift together the flour and baking powder. Add the sea salt. Using a rubber spatula, fold gently into the egg mixture. Add the lemon zest, then the brown butter.

Transfer the batter to an airtight container and refrigerate for at least 12 hours.

Fit the piping bag with a ¼-inch (.5-cm) nozzle tip. Spoon the batter into the piping bag and fill each madeleine mould with a rounded amount.

Bake for 15 minutes until the madeleines are golden on the top and spring back when gently pressed with the tip of your finger. Place on a cooling rack to cool.

Keep in an airtight container.

TIPS & TWISTS ....
Blend ⅛ tsp. (.5 mL) of crushed lavender seeds into the batter before baking.

EQUIPMENT ....
Electric mixer. Non-stick Madeleine pan. Zester. Medium size piping bag. Plastic spatula. Small sifter.

Peanut Butter "Peanuts" Spritz Cookies

{ MAKES 3 DOZEN }

Usually baked during the holidays, the delicate buttery crumble makes this
German traditional cookie a favourite year round. Now it's so very important to cream and
whip the batter to perfection. Otherwise you are going to get hand cramps trying to
squeeze that batter through a star tipped piping bag.

INSTRUCTIONS Preheat the oven to 360°F (180°C).

In an electric mixer bowl, using the paddle attachment cream together butter, peanut butter and sugar on medium speed. Use a rubber spatula to scrape the sides and bottom of the bowl to ensure the mixture is smooth. Add the egg, yolk and vanilla extract and beat on high speed for 1 minute.

Stir together the cake flour and baking powder. Add to the butter mixture and mix on low speed until the flour is completely incorporated into the dough. Dough should be soft. Transfer the dough to a piping bag fitted with star shape nozzle.

Pipe the dough into a twisted star shape, 2-inches (5-cm) apart on a parchment-lined baking sheet.

Press 2 pieces of peanut on the top of each piped cookie, sprinkle some sea salt, then dust with icing sugar using a small sieve.

Bake for 12 minutes until the edge of the cookies is lightly browned. Transfer to a cooling rack.

TIPS & TWISTS ....
Once baked and cooled, drizzle each cookie with melted dark or milk chocolate.

EQUIPMENT ....
Electric mixer. Rubber spatula. Small sieve. Piping bag. Large star shaped nozzle tip. Baking tray.

INGREDIENTS

½ cup (125 mL) unsalted butter

½ cup (125 mL) smooth peanut butter

½ cup (125 mL) light brown sugar

¼ cup (60 mL) granulated sugar

1 large egg

1 egg yolk

¼ tsp. (1.25 mL) vanilla extract

⅛ tsp. (.5 mL) baking soda

2 cups (500 mL) cake flour

TOPPING

¾ cup (180 mL) roasted peanuts

¼ cup (60 mL) icing sugar

1 tbsp. (15 mL) sea salt

Lemon Poppy Seed Butter Cookies

{ MAKES 2 DOZEN MEDIUM SIZE }

Always been a big fan of lemon poppy seed muffins? That was the first ever muffin recipe I ever made. I fell in love with that delightful combination and thought it would go well in a buttery cookie. Voila!

INGREDIENTS

1 cup (250 mL) unsalted butter

1 cup (250 mL) icing sugar

2 large eggs

½ tsp. (2.5 mL) sea salt

¾ tsp. (3.7 mL) baking soda

2½ cups (625 mL) all purpose flour

2 tsp. (10 mL) lemon zest

¼ cup (60 mL) poppy seeds

INSTRUCTIONS

Preheat the oven to 360°F (180°C).

In an electric mixer bowl, using the paddle attachment, cream the butter and icing sugar together. Mix until the texture is pale or about 6 minutes. Use a rubber spatula to scrape down the sides and bottom of the bowl to ensure the mixture is smooth. Add the eggs and continue mixing until fully incorporated.

Combine the flour, baking soda, salt, poppy seeds and lemon zest together and add to the butter mixture. Mix on low speed until the dough comes together. Empty the dough on a floured work surface.

Roll the dough into a log, ¾-inch (2-cm) in diagonal. Wrap in parchment paper and refrigerate for 2 hours.

Using a Chef knife, cut the log into ¼-inch (½-cm) thick rounds and place on a parchment-lined baking tray, each cookie being placed ½-inch (1-cm) apart. Using a small sieve, dust the top of each cookie with icing sugar.

Bake for 15 minutes or until the edge of the cookies is light brown in colour. Place the baking tray on a cooling rack.

TIPS & TWISTS ....
Replace the poppy seeds with ¼ cup (60 mL) sesame seeds.

EQUIPMENT ....
Electric mixer. Rubber spatula. Zester.

CHAPTER 4

Custards, Puddings & Mousses

Orange Blossom Flan

{ MAKES 6 }

The delicate aroma of orange blossom, combined with hints of caramel and the custard's silky texture, make this dessert a tasty treat. The added little touch of brown sugar gives it a subtle taste of molasses. Orange blossom is often associated with good fortune, so a happy day baking is always a triumph!

FOR THE CARAMEL Preheat the oven to 310°F (155°C). In a small saucepan, combine sugar and water. Place over medium heat until the sugar mixture starts to boil. Cook until sugar starts to colour into a light amber. Swirl gently but do not stir with a spoon or spatula to avoid the sugar crystalizing.

Quickly pour an equal amount into 4 ramekins, evenly coating the bottoms. Set aside to cool at room temperature.

In a medium saucepan, bring the cream to a boil.

FOR THE CUSTARD Meanwhile in a medium bowl, using a small hand whisk, mix together the eggs, egg yolks, both sugars and sea salt for about 1 minute. Slowly whisk the warm cream mixture into the eggs and stir until it is blended into a smooth custard. Pass through a fine mesh sieve. Place the ramekins into a water filled, deep-dish pan, and fill the ramekins with the custard mix.

Bake for about 35 minutes until the edge of the custard starts to colour into a light brown and the centre starts to jiggle. Remove from oven and place on a cooling rack still in the water-filled baking pan.

After 30 minutes, remove from the water-bath baking dish and place in a refrigerator for 6 hours.

Using a small paring knife, run the blade carefully around the sides of the ramekins to loosen the custard. Flip over on a small plate to unmould the custard.

TIPS & TWISTS ....
The orange blossom water can be easily substituted with rose petal water, or the cream infused with dried lavender.

EQUIPMENT ....
Small saucepan. Medium saucepan. Small hand whisk. 4 ramekins. Fine mesh sieve.

CARAMEL

½ cup (125 mL) granulated sugar

3 tbsp. (45 mL) water

CUSTARD

2 cups (500 mL) whipping cream

½ cup (125 mL) granulated sugar

2 tbsp (30 mL) light brown sugar

⅛ tsp. (.5 mL) sea salt

2 large eggs

3 large egg yolks

2 tsp. (10 mL) orange blossom water

A Very Lemony Lemon Curd

{ MAKES 2 CUPS (500 ML) }

A great lemon curd has the right balance between sweetness, a silky-smooth buttery texture and, of course, the right amount of zing that pops in the mouth in a fresh and joyful way. I found an easy and fun way to make this recipe: I use a microwave. It is delicious on its own, or makes a great filling for a lemon meringue tart, a choux paste, or for layering cakes.

INSTRUCTIONS Divide the sugar into 2 equal amounts and place in 2 glass bowls of 1 qt. (1 L) in size.

In one bowl, combine lemon juice, diced butter and half the sugar. Whisk well.

Place in a microwave and heat until it boils, using increments of 30 seconds cooking time.

In the other glass bowl, whisk the eggs and the remaining part of sugar until the mixture turns into a pale yellow colour. Pour the boiling lemon juice mixture on top of the whisked eggs. Stir until smooth. Return the mixture to the microwave, and cook, 30 seconds at a time, until the curd boils and thickens.

Pass the lemon curd through a fine mesh sieve. Allow to cool at room temperature. Place in an airtight container, covering the custard with a plastic wrap pressed onto the surface, then refrigerate until needed.

The lemon curd can last up to 10 days refrigerated.

TIPS & TWISTS ....

I love to add different types of zest like tangerine or lime to give the curd an extra pop of flavour. Also, to make not only Lemony but also Tipsy, I add ½ cup (125 mL) of Lemoncello Italian liqueur by whisking it in once the lemon curd is made and chilled.

EQUIPMENT ....

A small hand whisk. Fine mesh sieve. 2 glass bowls of 1 qt. (1 L) size.

INGREDIENTS

1 cup (250 mL) granulated sugar

4 large eggs

⅔ cup (160 mL) unsalted butter

¾ cup (180 mL) freshly squeezed lemon juice

Maple Sugar Crème Brûlée

{ MAKES 6 }

*A classic French dessert, crème brûlée has its origins in Spain where it is known
as Crema Catalana. In this version, I replaced the white granulated sugar with maple syrup.
White sugar is just boring. Take crème brûlée on a new tasty journey!*

INGREDIENTS

1 cup (250 mL) whipping cream

1 cup (250 mL) 10% cream

1¼ cups (310 mL) pure maple syrup

5 large egg yolks

½ cup (125 mL) raw sugar to caramelize the top of the custards just before serving

INSTRUCTIONS

Preheat the oven to 240°F (115°C).

In a medium saucepan, combine the whipping cream and 10% cream and bring to a boil.

Remove from heat.

Whisk together the maple syrup and egg yolks in a medium-size bowl. Pour the warm cream into the egg yolk mixture and stir well. Pass it through a fine mesh sieve to remove any cooked egg particles. Let rest for about 30 minutes at room temperature.

Place 4 ramekins (2-inches (5-cm) deep, 5-inches (12.5-cm) in diameter) into a deep dish filled with about 1½-inches (3.8-cm) of water. Place the dish in the oven and bake for about 40 minutes, or until the crème brûlée jiggles when shaken.

Remove the tray from the oven and place on a rack. Allow to cool then remove the ramekins from the water pan. Place on another tray and refrigerate for at least 6 hours.

When ready to serve, sprinkle a generous amount of sugar on the top. Using the broiler of your oven, slightly burn the top to create a caramel coating crust. You can also use a small propane torch available at most hardware stores.

TIPS & TWISTS

A crème brûlée is the perfect recipe to play with. As long as you keep the same ratio of sugar, egg yolks to the dairy components, it is easy to experiment with flavours.

EQUIPMENT

A small hand-whisk. Fine mesh sieve. 2 glass bowls of 1 qt. (1 L) size. Propane torch. 4 ramekins.

Italian Rice Pudding

{ MAKES 6 }

Being in a kitchen, a chef's mind is always at work playing around with ingredients,
imagining all sorts of variations of traditional recipes. Using Italian Arborio rice gives this pudding
a creamier texture and an earthier feel. It is a bit trickier to cook, but the result is worth it.
Served either warm or chilled, it has a light sweetness to it, and is simply delicious.

INSTRUCTIONS FOR THE CARAMEL Preheat the oven to 310°F (155°C).

In a small saucepan, combine sugar and water. Place over medium heat until the sugar mixture starts to boil and turns to a light amber colour. Swirl gently but do not stir with a spoon or spatula to avoid the sugar crystalizing.

Quickly pour an equal amount into 6 ramekins, evenly coating the bottoms. Set aside to cool at room temperature.

INSTRUCTIONS FOR THE RICE PUDDING In a medium saucepan, bring the rice to a boil in a cup of water and a pinch of sea salt and boil over low heat for about 15 minutes. Drain the water and set aside the cooked rice.

Meanwhile in a medium bowl, using a small hand whisk, combine the egg, egg yolks, sugar, Amaretto liquor and lemon zest. Slowly whisk in the milk and cream mixture and stir until it is blended into a smooth custard. Pass through a fine mesh sieve. Add the cooked rice to the mixture.

Fill the ramekins with the pudding and then place them in a water filled, deep-dish pan.

Bake for about 30 minutes until the edge of the puddings start to colour into a light brown and the centre starts to jiggle.

Remove from oven and place on a cooling rack still in the water-filled baking pan.

After 30 minutes, remove from the water-bath baking dish and place in a refrigerator for 6 hours. Using a small paring knife, run the blade carefully around the sides of the ramekins to loosen the custard. Flip over on a small plate to unmould each pudding.

TIPS & TWISTS ....

I love adding a tart component to this dessert, topping with fresh orange segments or fresh raspberries. For an alcohol-free option, use 1 tsp. (5 mL) of almond extract instead of Amaretto.

EQUIPMENT ....

Small saucepan. Medium bowl. Small hand whisk. 6 ramekins. Zester. Fine mesh sieve.

CARAMEL

½ cup (125 mL) granulated sugar

3 tbsp. (45 mL) water

RICE PUDDING

¼ cup (60 mL) Italian Arborio rice

1 cup (250 mL) whole milk

1 cup (250 mL) whipping cream

½ cup (125 mL) granulated sugar

1 large egg

2 large egg yolks

2 tbsp. (30 mL) Amaretto liquor

½ tsp. (2.5 mL) lemon zest

Cotton Candy Crème Brûlée

{ MAKES 6 }

*I know I will hear a lot of criticism from foul-mouthed chefs and diehard foodies
for using a blue-coloured junk food component in a recipe. But you can't beat the addictive nature of
cotton candy and the big smile it brings to people's faces. This recipe is evidence that things can get a little
crazy in the kitchen when too many creative minds get together. This dessert is just irresistible!*

INGREDIENTS

1 cup (250 mL) whipping cream

1 cup (250 mL) 10% cream

2 cups (500 mL) cotton candy

½ cup (125 mL) granulated sugar

5 large egg yolks

½ cup (125 mL) raw sugar to caramelize the top of the crème brûlée just before serving.

2 cups (250 mL) cotton candy for decoration

INSTRUCTIONS Preheat the oven to 240°F (115°C).

In a medium saucepan, bring both creams to a boil. Remove from heat.

Whisk together cotton candy, sugar and egg yolks in a medium-size bowl. Pour the warm cream into the egg yolk mixture and stir well. Pass it through a fine mesh sieve to remove any cooked egg bits.

Let rest for about 30 minutes at room temperature.

Place 4 ramekin dishes (ramekins should be ceramic, 2-inches (5-cm) deep, 5-inches (12.5-cm) in diameter) into a deep tray filled with about 1½-inches (3.8-cm) of water.

Place the pan in the oven and bake for about 40 minutes, or until the custard jiggles when shaken.

Remove the pan from the oven and place on a cooling rack. Allow the water to cool and then remove the ramekins. Place them on another tray and refrigerate for at least 6 hours.

When ready to serve, sprinkle a generous amount of sugar on the top. Using the broiler of your oven, slightly burn the top to create a caramel- crusted topping. You can also use a small propane torch available at hardware stores. Top with some of the remaining cotton candy for decoration.

TIPS & TWISTS ....

This recipe is funky enough. Don't change anything.

EQUIPMENT ....

A small hand whisk. Fine mesh sieve. 2 glass bowls of 1 qt. (1 L) size. Propane torch. 4 ramekin dishes.

Amaretto Mascarpone Mousse

{ MAKES 6 }

*Despite a German surname and a strong French accent, I grew up finding my way around a
kitchen with my Italian grandmother Louisa. I can also trace my family roots to Domenico Di Siena, a great great
grandfather born in 1785 in Santa Maria 'e Capua, a small Italian town south of Naples.*

*Rich in flavour, yet so light in texture, this dessert is a perfect way to warm up a winter's day by topping
it with poached fruits, or in summertime with sun-kissed berries.*

INSTRUCTIONS Using the electric mixer, with the whisk attachment,
beat the whipping cream into soft peaks. Transfer to a bowl and set aside
in the refrigerator until needed.

Still using the electric mixer, with the paddle attachment, on medium
speed combine the mascarpone cheese, icing sugar and orange zest until
smooth and creamy. Add the Amaretto liqueur. Transfer to a small bowl
and set aside.

Clean the electric mixing bowl thoroughly. Using the whisk attachment on the electric mixer, beat egg whites on medium speed. After
1 minute, gradually add the sugar, then increase the mixer to high speed
and beat until the egg whites form soft peaks. Using a rubber spatula,
gently fold the whipped egg whites into the mascarpone mixture, then
fold in the whipped cream.

Transfer to the tea cups, ¾ to the top, and refrigerate for at least
2 hours.

The mousse can be prepared 1 day ahead, and kept refrigerated.

TIPS & TWISTS ....
For an alcohol-free option, substitute Amaretto liqueur with 1 tsp. (5 mL)
of pure almond extract. Delicious when you drizzle an espresso on the
top. Or served with one of the biscotti recipes found in Chapter 3.

EQUIPMENT ....
Electric mixer. 6 teacups. Small hand whisk. 2 medium bowls. 1 medium
bowl. Rubber spatula. Zester.

INGREDIENTS

1 cup (250 mL) mascarpone
cheese

¼ cup (60 mL) icing sugar

½ tsp. (2.5 mL) orange zest

2 tbsp. (30 mL) Amaretto
liqueur

¼ cup (60 mL) egg whites

¼ cup (60 mL) granulated
sugar

1 cup (250 mL) whipping
cream

Milk Chocolate Espresso Mousse

{ MAKES 6 }

The choice of milk chocolate brand is important. It will bring great flavour and a smooth texture. I prefer a high quality European or small-batch, artisan chocolate made in North America.

INSTRUCTIONS Beat the whipping cream into soft peaks. Set aside in the refrigerator until needed.

Pour the cream and the milk into a small saucepan, and bring to a quick boil. Stir the instant coffee into the heated liquid.

Place the milk chocolate into a medium bowl, and pour in the hot coffee-infused milk and cream. Gently stir until the chocolate is melted, and the texture is smooth.

Wait a few minutes until the chocolate mixture is lukewarm. Gently fold in the soft peaked whipped cream using a rubber spatula. Do not fold the whipped cream too soon or it will melt.

Transfer to the Mason jars, filling ¾ to the top, and refrigerate for at least 2 hours.

The mousse can be prepared up to 2 days ahead of serving.

TIPS & TWISTS ....

You can double the amount of instant coffee and call it a double espresso, milk chocolate mousse. Delicious served frozen. Pour some warm chocolate sauce on the top, and eat it like a semifreddo. Or try topping it with an amazing dark and silky chocolate sauce (recipe, page 37). Or sprinkled with some diced candied ginger.

EQUIPMENT ....

6 medium-size Mason jars. Small hand whisk. Medium size pan. Rubber spatula

INGREDIENTS

½ cup (125 mL) 10% cream

½ cup (125 mL) whole milk

½ tbsp. (7.5 mL) instant coffee

2 cups (500 mL) milk chocolate, chopped into small pieces

1 cup (250 mL) whipping cream

Chocolate Orange Soufflé

{ MAKES 6 }

A classic 18th-century, warm French dessert, this soufflé is loved all over the world.
Its preparation will often make inexperienced bakers a bit nervous, but this almost-fool-proof
recipe will make you feel like a star baker. However, full disclosure, even after 35 years of professional
baking experience, I do indeed still feel nervous when I make a soufflé. And for once,
I am using salted butter in the recipe just to add a slight umami taste to it.

INGREDIENTS

½ cup (125 mL) chopped extra bitter chocolate

1 tbsp. (15 mL) cocoa powder

3 egg yolks

⅓ cup (80 mL) salted butter

½ tsp. (2.5 mL) instant coffee

½ tsp. (2.5 mL) orange zest

6 egg whites

⅓ cup (80 mL) granulated sugar

COATING FOR THE RAMEKINS

2 tbsp. (30 mL) soft unsalted butter

4 tbsp. (60 mL) granulated sugar

Using 2 tbsp. (30 mL) of soft butter, grease the whole inside of the four ramekins. Then coat the inside with granulated sugar.

INSTRUCTIONS Preheat the oven to 380°F (195°C)

Melt the chocolate in a double boiler or bain-marie. Stir with a wooden spoon until completely melted.

Remove from the heat, then stir in the butter, orange zest, instant coffee, cocoa powder and lastly, the egg yolks.

In the electric mixer, using the whisk attachment, beat the egg whites until they start to foam, gradually adding the remaining ½ (125 mL) cup of sugar. Beat on high speed until soft peaks form.

Use a rubber spatula to gently fold the whipped egg whites into the chocolate mixture.

Transfer to the ramekins filling them 90% up to the rim.

Bake for approximately 22 minutes, or until the soufflés have risen and the top looks slightly dry.

Remove from the oven, dust the top with a generous amount of icing sugar and serve right away, otherwise it will start to slowly deflate after 2 minutes.

TIPS & TWISTS ....
Serve with a scoop of vanilla ice cream on the side. Dig your spoon into the warm soufflé then scoop some ice cream. The combination of the light warm texture of the soufflé with the cold creamy ice cream is magical.

EQUIPMENT ....
Six 3.5-in. (8.9-cm) soufflé ramekins. Electric mixer. Rubber spatula. Small hand whisk. Medium bowl. Large bowl.

Cranberry Clafouti

{ MAKES ONE 8-INCH (20-CM) TART }

A quintessential baked French dessert, it traditionally is made with dark cherries. I love how the flavours of the juicy, sour cranberries play with the lightly sweetened, creamy custard.

INSTRUCTIONS Preheat the oven to 325°F (160°C).

In a medium bowl, using a hand whisk, mix the eggs, sugar, flour, cinnamon, vanilla extract and orange zest. Once combined, whisk in the milk and sour cream.

Arrange the cranberries at the bottom of an 8-inch (20-cm) ceramic pie dish. Pour the batter over the top of the cranberries.

Bake for 1 hour, until the edges are slightly brown, but still soft in the centre. Remove from the oven, and dust the entire surface with icing sugar using a small sifter.

Serve warm.

TIPS & TWISTS ....
Substitute the cranberries with the same amount of blueberries.

EQUIPMENT ....
One 8-inch (20-cm) ceramic pie dish. Medium bowl. Hand whisk. Small sieve.

INGREDIENTS

2 cups (500 mL) fresh cranberries

4 large eggs

1 cup (250 mL) whole milk

¼ cup (60 mL) sour cream

¼ cup (60 mL) granulated sugar

1 tsp. (5 mL) orange zest

¼ tsp. (1.25 mL) ground cinnamon

¼ cup (60 mL) cake flour

1 tsp. (5 mL) vanilla extract

¼ cup (60 mL) icing sugar (for decoration)

Chocolate "Figgy" Pudding

{ MAKES ONE 8-INCH (20-CM) ROUND, DEEP BAKING DISH }

There is a misconception that the French make the best desserts. People in every nation have a sweet tooth, including Brits. A rustic, warm English dessert, it is enjoyable at any time of the year—especially if topped with stewed, fresh peach compote.

INGREDIENTS

¼ cup (60 mL) unsalted butter

½ cup (125 mL) granulated sugar

2 large eggs

1 tsp. (5 mL) vanilla extract

½ cup (125 mL) cocoa powder

½ cup (125 mL) chopped dark chocolate

½ cup (125 mL) ground almonds

2 cups cake flour

½ tsp. (2.5 mL) sea salt

¼ tsp. (1.25 mL) baking soda

1 cup (250 mL) whole milk

2 cups (500 mL) dried figs

¼ cup (60 mL) brandy (optional)

INSTRUCTIONS

Preheat oven to 360°F (180°C)

Remove the stems of the dried figs and cut the fruit into quarters.

In an electric mixer, using the paddle attachment, cream together the butter and sugar until smooth. Add the eggs and vanilla extract and keep mixing on medium speed until smooth. Use a rubber spatula to scrape down the sides of the bowl. Add the cocoa powder, chocolate, ground almonds and brandy. Mix on low speed until fully incorporated.

In another bowl, combine flour, salt and baking soda. Take turns adding the flour and the milk into the butter and sugar mixture. Stir in the figs. Pour batter into a greased deep, 8-inch (20-cm) round ceramic pan.

Place in a deep-dish, water bath. Cover with tin foil.

Bake for 1 hour.

Once out of the oven, remove the tin foil but leave the dish in the water bath. Allow to cool for 20 minutes and then remove the pudding from the water bath. Allow it to cool for another 20 minutes. Unmould the pudding onto a platter.

Best served warm with a scoop of vanilla ice cream.

TIPS & TWISTS ....

Substitute the dried figs with dried apricots or dried sour cherries.

EQUIPMENT ....

Electric mixer. Large bowl. Rubber spatula. 8-inch (20-cm) round deep ceramic pan. Deep dish tray.

Raspberry Mousse

{ SERVES 4 }

*A fruit mousse is the perfect recipe to highlight a seasonal fruit at the peak of its season.
The idea is to blend an acidic fruit pulp and a creamy light component. This delicious summer
dessert can be topped with fresh berries and biscotti.*

INSTRUCTIONS In an electric mixer, using the whisk attachment, whip the cream until soft peaks form. Set aside in the refrigerator until needed.

In a tall blender, mix the raspberries, sugar and lemon juice until smooth on medium speed. Remove all the seeds by passing the raspberry purée through a fine mesh sieve.

Dissolve the gelatine powder with 4 tbsp. (60 mL) of cold water and stir with a small spoon until smooth. Pour the raspberry purée into a medium saucepan and warm slightly. It should feel warm to the touch.

Remove from the stove then whisk in the dissolved gelatine. Gently fold the whipped cream into the purée until fully incorporated and spoon the raspberry mousse equally into 4 glasses.

Refrigerate for 2 hours before serving.

TIPS & TWISTS ....
Easily substitute the raspberries with strawberries. Or create a two-flavour combination by alternating layers of raspberry mousse and lemon curd for a delicious summer dessert.

EQUIPMENT ....
Electric mixer. Medium saucepan. Rubber spatula. Hand whisk. Small sieve. Tall blender.

INGREDIENTS

2 cups (500 mL) fresh or frozen raspberries

¾ cup (60 mL) icing sugar

2 tbsp. (30 mL) lemon juice

1 tbsp. (15 mL) unflavoured gelatine

1½ cups (375 mL) whipping cream

Honey Buttermilk Panna Cotta

{ MAKES 4 }

*Panna Cotta is an eggless Italian custard. I have made panna cottas
with more flavour variations than I can remember. Silky, creamy and dreamy. This is how
I describe this easy-to-make Italian dessert.*

INGREDIENTS

1½ cups (375 mL) whipping
cream

½ cup (125 mL) buttermilk

¼ cup (60 mL) honey

½ tsp. (2.5 mL) vanilla extract

1 tbsp. (15 mL) unflavoured
gelatine

¼ cup (60 mL) milk

INSTRUCTIONS

Place milk in a small bowl and sprinkle gelatine. Using a fork, stir and let rest for 5-10 minutes to soften.

In a medium saucepan, heat cream, honey and vanilla extract on medium heat up to a boiling point. Remove from heat and whisk in the gelatine.

In a small saucepan slightly warm the buttermilk then pour over the cream mixture. Stir well.

Place the glasses on a baking sheet. Pour the panna cotta mixture into the glasses.

Refrigerate for 4 hours.

TIPS & TWISTS ....
Top with seasonal berries.

EQUIPMENT ....
Small saucepan. Small bowl. Small hand whisk. 4 medium mason jars.

Frozen Lemon Soufflé

{ SERVES 4 }

This easy-to-make frozen dessert is bursting with lemony flavour—
a refreshing dessert for hot summer days.

INSTRUCTIONS In an electric mixer, using the whisk attachment, beat the egg whites on medium speed.

As the egg whites start to foam, gradually add the sugar while increasing the whisking speed. Whip until the egg whites become soft peaks. Transfer the whipped egg whites to a medium bowl and set aside.

Pour the whipping cream into the electric mixer bowl, and using the whisk attachment, whip until soft peaks form.

Fold the lemon zest into the whipped egg whites, then gently fold in the whipped cream.

Spoon the mixture into four 1-cup Mason jars (250 mL) and place in the freezer for 2 hours.

Top with berries or whipped cream before serving.

TIPS & TWISTS ....
Substitute the lemon zest with 2 tsp. (10 mL) of ground coriander; unusual, but refreshingly delicious.

EQUIPMENT ....
Electric mixer. Medium Bowl. Rubber spatula. Zester.

INGREDIENTS

½ cup (125 mL) egg whites

½ cup (125 mL) granulated sugar

1½ cups (375 mL) whipping cream

4 tsp. (20 mL) lemon zest

Chocolate Pot de Crème

{ MAKES 6 }

I first starting making Chocolate Pot de Crème while working in New York.
One of my assistants shared with me this delicious recipe. Though not quite as popular or
well known as its cousin Crème Brûlée, Pot De Crème is a lush and velvety dessert.

INGREDIENTS

2 cups (500 mL) whipping cream

½ cup (125 mL) whole milk

3 tbsp. (45 mL) granulated sugar

4 egg yolks

⅛ tsp. (.5 mL) sea salt

⅔ cup (160 mL) 64% dark chocolate, chopped

INSTRUCTIONS

Preheat the oven to 240°F (115°C).

In a saucepan, bring to a boil the cream and milk. Remove from heat.

In a medium bowl, using a hand whisk, beat sugar, egg yolks and sea salt until the mixture turns a pale yellow colour. Add the chopped dark chocolate to the sugar and egg mixture. Pour the boiling cream on top and using a hand whisk stir gently until the chocolate is melted and the mixture is smooth. Pass through a sieve.

Place the 6 ceramic dishes into a deep, water-filled pan. Pour the chocolate mixture into the 6 ceramic dishes, almost to the top.

Bake for 30 minutes or until the chocolate custard starts to firm and feels like jelly. Remove from oven and place on a cooling rack. Once cooled, remove each ceramic dish from the water.

Place in a refrigerator for 1 hour.

Best served topped with fresh raspberries and a dollop of whipped cream.

TIPS & TWISTS ....
Add ½ tsp. (2.5 mL) ground cinnamon to the boiling cream.

EQUIPMENT ....
Hand whisk. Medium bowl. Medium saucepan. Small sieve. 6 ceramic dishes 1 cup (250 mL) each.

CHAPTER 5

Cakes, Tarts, Loaves, Pies & Cheesecakes

Rhubarb & Sweet Cherry Buckwheat Crisp

{ MAKES ONE 8-INCH (20-CM) PIE }

After a long cold winter, our moods always brighten at the thought
of summer fruits—particularly cherries. Combined with rhubarb and topped
with a flavourful buckwheat crumble, it makes for a delicious dessert.

INSTRUCTIONS Preheat the oven to 360°F (180°C).

In a large bowl, combine diced rhubarb, thawed cherries, both sugars, vanilla extract, corn starch and flour. Using a rubber spatula, fold continuously until all the fruit pieces are coated. Transfer the mix into an 8-inch (20-cm) pie plate. Top with Buckwheat Crumble topping, covering the entire surface.

Bake for 40 minutes or until the top is golden in colour and you see the fruit juices bubbling on the edge of the cobbler. Remove from the oven and place on a cooling rack.

Crisp is best served slightly warm or at room temperature.

TIPS & TWISTS ....
Substitute the rhubarb with fresh juicy peaches or apricots, but keep the cherries.

EQUIPMENT ....
Large bowl. Medium bowl. Rubber spatula. 8-inch (20-cm) round ceramic pie plate.

INGREDIENTS

2 cups (500 mL) frozen sweet cherries (pitted)

1½ cups (375 mL) diced fresh rhubarb

¼ cup (60 mL) granulated sugar

½ cup (125 mL) light brown sugar

1 tbsp. (15 mL) vanilla extract

1½ tbsp. (22 mL) corn starch

2 tsp. (10 mL) cake flour

1 recipe Buckwheat crumble topping (See page 42)

Double Chocolate Angel Food Cake

{ SERVES 8 }

One of the most delightful desserts ever created, Angel food cake originated in the early 1800s, most likely from around Pennsylvania. This dessert really reinforces the idea that North America has a long baking tradition.

The secret for creating the beautiful light, almost airy texture of an angel food cake is to not grease the inside of the mould.

CAKE BATTER

1½ tbsp. (22 mL) cocoa powder

3 tbsp. (45 mL) water

1 cup (240 mL) granulated sugar

1 tsp. (5 mL) orange zest

¼ tsp. (1.25 mL) cardamom powder

1 cup (250 mL) cake flour

½ tsp. (2.5 mL) sea salt

1½ cups (375 mL) egg whites

½ cup (125 mL) granulated sugar

CHOCOLATE GLAZE

½ cup (125 mL) evaporated milk

¼ cup (60 mL) condensed milk

¼ cup (60 mL) light corn syrup

¼ cup (60 mL) granulated sugar

½ cup (125 mL) extra bitter chocolate

¼ cup (60 mL) unsalted butter

INSTRUCTIONS FOR THE CAKE Preheat the oven to 360°F (180°C).

In a small bowl, combine water, cocoa powder and orange zest together. Sift together 1 cup of the sugar, flour, cardamom and sea salt into a bowl.

Using the electric mixer with the whisk attachment, whip the egg whites until foamy, gradually adding the remaining ½ cup sugar whipping until stiff peaks form. Whisk a large spoonful of whipped egg whites into the chocolate mixture, then gently fold it back into the whipped egg whites. Using the rubber spatula, gradually fold the sifted, dry ingredients into the whipped egg whites, quickly but gently to avoid deflating the whipped egg whites. Spoon the cake batter into a 10-inch (25-cm) ungreased tube cake mould.

Place on the lower rack of the oven and bake for 45 minutes. The cake is done when it springs back when touched. The cake will also have cracks in the top.

Remove from oven, run a long-blade knife around the edges of the cake mould, including the centre. Place a cooling rack on top of the cake, and quickly invert by flipping the cake over. Leave the cake in the mould and let it cool at room temperature for 1 hour. Loosen the mould to remove.

Place on a serving plate, and drizzle the top with the chocolate glaze.

FOR THE GLAZE In a medium saucepan, bring evaporated and condensed milk to a boil. Remove from heat, then add corn syrup, sugar and chocolate. Stir well with a hand whisk. Place back on the stove over low heat, and while stirring, bring back to a boil and cook for 2 minutes. Pass through a fine mesh sieve. Whisk in the butter and whisk until the glaze is smooth. Pour onto the entire cake right before serving.

TIPS & TWISTS ....
Add 2 tbsp. (30 mL) of instant coffee to the cocoa mixture.

EQUIPMENT ....
Electric mixer. Large bowl. Medium bowl. Small bowl. 10-inch (25.4-cm) tube cake mould. Fine mesh sieve. Rubber spatula. Medium saucepan. Small hand whisk.

Chocolate Mocha Swiss Rolls

{ SERVES 8 }

This chocolate cake is rich and decadent, and a lovely treat for all chocolate lovers.
Of course, being a chocolate lover myself, I even indulge in it for breakfast (actually, often to be honest).
It is the best way to start your day.

INSTRUCTIONS FOR CHOCOLATE ROULADE SPONGE Preheat oven to 350°F (175°C).

Sift together flour, cocoa powder, corn starch and baking soda. Place the eggs in a bain-marie (see Glossary page 12) with simmering water. Add sugar to the eggs in a stream while beating the eggs. Whisk by hand until the egg and sugar mixture becomes warm.

Place batter into an electric mixer bowl, then whisk on high speed until batter becomes light and fluffy with a ribbon consistency. Remove bowl from mixer, then, with a rubber spatula, gently fold the dry ingredients into the whipped eggs. Using an offset spatula, spread evenly onto a parchment-lined baking tray.

Bake for about 20 minutes. Remove from the oven and place on cooling rack. Once cool, cover with a clean kitchen towel to keep the sponge moist.

INSTRUCTIONS FOR MOCHA GANACHE Melt the chocolate in a bain-marie.

In a small saucepan, bring the milk to a boil. Remove from stove, whisk in instant coffee and let infuse for 3 minutes. Pour on top of melted chocolate. Stir gently until smooth. Remove from bain-marie and let cool for 1 hour.

ASSEMBLY Using a small hand-whisk, mix the mocha ganache to a soft consistency.

Place chocolate sponge on a flat working surface. Spread the soft mocha ganache evenly all over the sponge. Tightly fold one end of the sponge into a roll, while at the same time removing the parchment paper. Place on a baking tray and freeze the cake for 30 minutes.

Place the roll on a cutting board and, using a slicing knife, slice gently into 1-inch (2.5-cm) or slightly wider (3-cm) portions. Place on a platter and dust with icing sugar.

TIPS & TWISTS ....

Right before rolling the sponge, sprinkle brandied cherries that have been drained from their macerating juice.

EQUIPMENT ....

Electric mixer. Large bowl. Rubber spatula. Fine mesh sieve. Small hand whisk. Medium offset spatula. Small saucepan. Small bowl. Slicing knife.

CHOCOLATE ROULADE SPONGE

4 large eggs

½ cup (125 mL) granulated sugar

½ cup (125 mL) all purpose flour

¼ cup (60 mL) cocoa powder

2 tbsp. (30 mL) corn starch

⅛ tsp. (.5 mL) baking soda

MOCHA GANACHE

1½ cup (375 mL) extra bitter chocolate

1 cup (250 mL) whole milk

1 tbsp. (5 mL) instant coffee

Olive Oil Semolina Cake

{ ONE 8-INCH (20-CM) ROUND CAKE }

This is one of the easier cakes to make. So don't let the name intimidate you.
It has a nice crumble and lovely light sweetness. Use a fruity extra-virgin olive oil, so its aromas carry
through the bake. And yes, the combined 2 cups of olive oil and butter make it a delicious cake.
By now, you will have understood how much I love butter.

INGREDIENTS

1¼ cup (310 mL) all-purpose flour

¾ cup (180 mL) semolina

½ cup (125 mL) light brown sugar, packed

½ cup (125. mL) granulated sugar

2 tsp. (10 mL) baking powder

1 tsp. (5 mL) sea salt

4 large eggs

1 cup (250 mL) extra virgin olive oil

1 cup (250 mL) unsalted melted butter

¼ cup (60 mL) icing sugar to dust the top of the cake batter before baking

INSTRUCTIONS

Preheat the oven to 360°F (180°C).

Line a baking pan with parchment paper.

In a large bowl, using a hand whisk beat the eggs and the granulated sugar until they fluff into a pale yellow colour.

In another bowl, mix together the all purpose flour, light brown sugar, baking powder, semolina and sea salt. Fold the dry ingredients mixture into the fluffy eggs, then add the olive oil and lastly the melted butter. Continue folding the mixture until smooth. Pour the cake batter into the prepared baking tray, making sure the cake batter is spread evenly.

Using a small fine mesh sieve, dust the icing sugar over the top of all the cake batter. Place on the middle rack of the oven.

Bake for 20 minutes at 360°F (180°C) Rotate the baking tray 180 degrees to ensure an even bake.

Bake for another 10 minutes at the same temperature. Remove from oven and place on a cooling rack.

Once the cake has cooled, it is ready to enjoy.

TIPS & TWISTS

This cake is so versatile, crumble it on top of a scoop of vanilla ice cream or raspberry sorbet, or cut into finger size morsels to dip into a delicious lemon curd. Or add sliced fresh basil leaves to the cake batter before pouring on the baking sheet, to make this Olive Oil Semolina Cake molto Italiano. The dusting of icing sugar before the bake creates a beautiful delicate glaze effect.

EQUIPMENT

8-inch round (20-cm) spring mould. Medium size hand whisk. Medium bowls. Rubber spatula. Small sieve.

Maple Syrup Pound Cake

{ MAKES 1 LOAF }

This is a Canadian version of a cake I tasted during a trip to New Orleans.
The original recipe asked for Steen's pure cane syrup. Using pure maple syrup gives it an amazing
flavour boost! Dunk into café au lait and ooh la la!

INSTRUCTIONS Preheat the oven to 360°F (180°C).

In an electric mixing bowl, using the paddle attachment, cream together the butter and sugar at medium speed. Use a plastic spatula to scrape down the sides and bottom of the bowl to ensure a smooth texture. Add the eggs and mix until fully incorporated. Add the maple syrup very slowly to avoid the batter splitting.

In a small bowl, stir together the flour, baking soda, baking powder and sea salt. With the electric mixer powered off, pour all the dry ingredients into the batter, then mix on low speed until all is incorporated. Do not over mix.

Grease the inside of the loaf pan. Pour the cake batter into the loaf pan and place it on a small baking sheet. Position the sheet on the middle rack of the oven.

Bake for 45 minutes at 360°F (180°C). Insert a toothpick or a small knife blade into the middle of the cake to check that the cake is baked through. It should come out clean. Remove from the oven and place on rack to cool.

FOR THE GLAZE In a small bowl, stir together water, icing sugar and lemon zest until smooth. Using a pastry brush, apply to the top of the pound cake while it is still warm.

TIPS & TWISTS ....
This cake is a great base for other desserts: add fruit such as diced fresh apple or fresh blueberries to the batter before baking.

EQUIPMENT ....
Electric mixer. Plastic spatula. Zester. Pastry brush. Loaf pan.

INGREDIENTS

½ cup (125 mL) unsalted butter

½ cup (125 mL) granulated sugar

1 cup (250 mL) pure maple syrup

1½ tsp. (7 mL) baking powder

½ tsp. (2.5 mL) baking soda

¼ tsp. (1.25 mL) sea salt

2 eggs

2¼ cups (560 mL) all-purpose flour

FOR THE GLAZE

¼ cup (60 mL) lemon juice

¾ cup (180 mL) icing sugar

1 tsp. (5 mL) lemon zest

Flourless Almond Chocolate Cake

{ MAKES ONE 10-INCH (25-CM) ROUND }

Rich and moist, I love this cake for its simplicity and deep chocolate flavour.
Best served warm.

INGREDIENTS

¾ cup (180 mL) unsalted butter

¼ cup (60 mL) icing sugar

12 egg yolks

1 cup (125 mL) finely ground almonds

¼ tsp. (1.25 mL) sea salt

1¼ cups (310 mL) dark chocolate, chopped, melted over bain marie (see Glossary page 12) and kept warm

10 large egg whites

½ cup (125 mL) granulated sugar

INSTRUCTIONS

Preheat the oven to 360°F (180°C).

In an electric mixing bowl, with the paddle attachment, cream together the butter, sea salt and sugar. Add the egg yolks one at a time, scraping down the sides of the bowl from time to time to ensure a smooth texture. Transfer the butter mixture to a large bowl, cover with plastic wrap, and set aside at room temperature.

Wash the mixing bowl thoroughly with soapy water to remove any traces of fat. Using the whisk attachment, beat the egg whites until foamy, then gradually add the sugar, beating into soft peaks. Using the rubber spatula, fold the melted chocolate and ground almonds into the butter mixture. Next, gently fold in the whipped egg whites.

Spoon the cake batter almost to the top into a greased and floured cake pan.

Bake for 20 minutes. Use the blade of a small knife to check if the cake is cooked enough. The blade should come out clean. The centre of the cake needs to feel undercooked to keep its lovely moist texture. Remove from the oven and place on a cooling rack.

TIPS & TWISTS ....
Once the cake is baked and ready to serve, drizzle some Kahlua or Bailey's on each serving. Delicious served with a scoop of coffee ice cream.

EQUIPMENT ....
Electric mixer. 10-inch (25.4-cm) round spring-form cake pan. Small bowl. Large bowl. Rubber spatula.

Candy Cane Cheesecake

{ SERVES 8 | MAKES ONE 8-INCH (20-CM) ROUND }

Taking a classic North American dessert and giving it a festive spin is one of my favourite ways to switch things up. In this case with cheesecake, I've added crushed candy canes. I just love how the peppermint pops in the mouth, and how the melted candy canes swirl into the cheesecake as it bakes. The base of the cheesecake also gets a holiday makeover with the addition of ginger and cinnamon.

INSTRUCTIONS FOR THE BASE Preheat the oven to 360°F (180°C).

In a medium bowl, mix by hand the ground graham crackers, light brown sugar, ground cinnamon and the ground ginger. Add the melted butter and stir until combined.

Transfer the base mixture to a parchment-lined and greased 8-inch (20-cm), springform pan.

Bake for 15 minutes. Remove from oven and allow to cool at room temperature.

INSTRUCTIONS FOR THE CAKE Lower the oven temperature to 260°F (125°C)

In an electric mixer bowl, with the paddle attachment, mix the cream cheese at low speed until soft. Add the brown sugar, eggs and lastly, the sour cream. Be sure the mixture is smooth and lump free. Pass through a fine mesh sieve. Once the batter is free of any lumps, gently fold in the crushed candy canes. Fill the cake pan and place on a baking sheet.

Bake for about 35 minutes at 260°F (125°C).

TIPS & TWISTS ....

Make this cheesecake even richer by substituting half the cream cheese with ricotta cheese..

EQUIPMENT ....

Electric mixer. 8-inch (20-cm) round springform cake mould. Rubber spatula. Fine mesh sieve.

FOR THE BASE

1½ cups (375 mL) ground graham crackers

⅓ cup (80 mL) light brown sugar

6 tbsp. (90 mL) unsalted butter

½ tsp. (2.5 mL) ground ginger

½ tsp. (2.5 mL) ground cinnamon

CANDY CANE CHEESECAKE

2½ cups (625 mL) cream cheese

¾ cup (180 mL) light brown sugar

2 large eggs

½ cup (125 mL) sour cream

1 cup (250 mL) crushed candy canes

Gateau à la Tomate

{ SERVES 8 | MAKES ONE 8-INCH (20-CM) ROUND }

Having such a curious mind, I love when home cooks share family recipes with me.
Françoise Gingras' daughter asked me to try this century-old recipe from Quebec. It is simply delicious.
The trick is to use canned tomato soup.

INGREDIENTS

½ cup (125 mL) unsalted butter

2 large eggs

1 cup (250 mL) granulated sugar

1½ cups (375 mL) all purpose flour

1 tsp. (5 mL) ground cinnamon

½ tsp. (2.5 mL) ground cloves

¾ cup (180 mL) dried cranberries

½ tsp. (2.5 mL) baking powder

One 10-oz. (296 mL) small can of condensed tomato soup

INSTRUCTIONS Preheat the oven to 360°F (180°C).

Cut an 8-inch (20-cm) round of parchment paper and place at the base of an 8-inch (20-cm) springform cake pan.

In an electric mixer bowl, using the paddle attachment, cream together the butter and sugar. Once the mixture is creamy, add the eggs. Use a rubber spatula to scrape down the sides of the bowl. Be sure the mixture is smooth, free of butter lumps.

In a medium bowl, stir together flour, baking powder, cinnamon, cloves and dried cranberries. Add the can of tomato soup to the butter mixture. Mix well on low speed to ensure soup is completely blended into the batter. Add the flour mixture and mix just enough for the batter to come together. Pour the batter into the cake pan. Place on the middle rack of the oven.

Bake for 25 minutes at 360°F (180°C) Rotate the baking tray 180 degrees to ensure an even bake.

Bake for another 20 minutes at the same temperature. Remove from the oven and place on a cooling rack. Once the cake has cooled, unmould and place on a serving platter.

The cake is very moist and delicious on its own.

TIPS & TWISTS ....

Don't change anything. No one wants to mess with Françoise.

EQUIPMENT...

Electric mixer. 8-inch (20-cm) round cake springform. Medium bowl. Rubber spatula.

Chocolate Raspberry Cake in a Mug

{ MAKES 4 }

Easy to make and so yummy, this warm chocolate cake can be prepared in less than 15 minutes—from weighing the ingredients to baking. I often create a competition with friends, timer in hand. Who can make it the fastest?

INSTRUCTIONS In a bowl, stir together flour, sugar, cocoa powder, baking powder and sea salt.

In another bowl, melt the butter in the microwave. Stir canola oil and milk into the melted butter. Whisk the wet mixture into dry ingredients. Fold in the chocolate chips and the raspberries. Spoon the batter into the coffee mugs until ¾ full.

Microwave for about 90 seconds on high. Do not over cook. The cake is better undercooked. Let cool down for 2 minutes.

Top with the remaining raspberries and a spoonful of crème fraiche or sour cream.

TIPS & TWISTS ....
Substitute white chocolate with dark chocolate and add ¼ cup of raspberry liqueur.

The cakes bake better in a mug with a wider opening.

EQUIPMENT ....
Mixing bowl. Hand whisk. Rubber spatula. 4 microwave-safe coffee mugs. Microwave.

INGREDIENTS

1 cup (250 mL) all-purpose flour

¾ cup (180 mL) granulated sugar

½ cup (125 mL) cocoa powder

1½ tsp. (7.5 mL) baking powder

½ tsp. (2.5 mL) sea salt

½ cup (125 mL) white chocolate chips

¾ cup (180 mL) milk

½ cup (125 mL) unsalted butter

¼ cup (60 mL) canola oil

½ pint (125 mL) fresh raspberries

½ cup (125 mL) crème fraiche or sour cream for topping

½ pint (125 mL) fresh raspberries for garnish

Warm Blueberry Crisp

{ MAKES ONE 8-INCH (20-CM) PIE }

*I arrived in the U.S. in 1988, and until then I had never heard of desserts called crisps
or cobblers. After a week of discovering and wandering the streets of New York City, I stepped into
a bookstore and found a book that immediately captivated me: The American Baker by Jim Dodge.
It was a revelation. I was like 'wow,' they have bakers in America! And right there were the recipes
and the inspiration for many desserts—all tasty, with real soul. I fell in love with that book.*

INGREDIENTS

4 cups (1 L) fresh or frozen blueberries

¼ cup (60 mL) orange juice

½ cup (125 mL) granulated sugar

⅓ cup (80 mL) light brown sugar

2 tbsp. (60 mL) corn starch

3 tbsp. (45 mL) unsalted butter

1 tsp. (5 mL) lemon zest

1 tsp. (5 mL) vanilla extract

1 recipe of Brown Sugar Oats Streusel (see page 34)

INSTRUCTIONS Preheat the oven to 360°F (180°C).

Melt the butter. Place berries, orange juice, both sugars, corn starch, lemon zest and vanilla extract in a bowl. Using a rubber spatula gently toss until all the blueberries are coated with all the ingredients. Transfer blueberry mixture into a ceramic pie dish.

Top the entire surface with the brown sugar oats streusel.

Bake for approximately 40 minutes or until the top has a nice light brown colour. Remove from the oven and place on a cooling rack.

Best served while still warm.

TIPS & TWISTS ....
Serve with a scoop of vanilla or salted caramel ice cream.

EQUIPMENT ....
Large bowl. Medium bowl. Rubber spatula. 8-inch (20-cm) round ceramic pie dish.

Pumpkin, Date & Nut Loaf

{ MAKES 1 LOAF }

The pumpkin purée in the recipe keeps this loaf moist and is a nutritious and delicious snack for all the "kids" in the family.

INSTRUCTIONS Preheat the oven to 360°F (180°C).

Butter the inside of a loaf pan.

In a bowl, using a hand whisk, stir together flour, baking soda, nutmeg, sea salt and cinnamon.

In an electric mixer bowl, using the paddle attachment, combine pumpkin purée and sugars on low speed. After 1 minute, add the eggs and mix for about 2 minutes. Once the eggs are fully incorporated, add the honey, oil, corn syrup and apple juice. Then add the flour mixture and mix for another minute on low speed. Use a rubber spatula to scrape down the sides of the bowl to ensure all the ingredients are fully incorporated. Remove the bowl from the mixer, and using the rubber spatula, fold in the dates and nuts. Pour the batter into the greased loaf pan.

Bake for 40 minutes. Insert the blade of a small knife in the middle of the loaf to check that it's baked completely. The blade should come out clean.

TIPS & TWISTS ....

Substitute dates with diced candied ginger.

EQUIPMENT ....

Electric mixer. Plastic spatula. Hand whisk. Medium bowl. Cake loaf pan.

INGREDIENTS

2 cups (500 mL) pumpkin purée

¾ cup (180 mL) granulated sugar

¼ cup (60 mL) light brown sugar

3 eggs

2 tbsp. (30 mL) honey

½ cup (125 mL) canola oil

¼ cup (60 mL) light corn syrup

½ cup (125 mL) apple juice

2 tsp. (10 mL) baking soda

1 tsp. (5 mL) baking powder

¼ tsp. (1.25 mL) nutmeg

½ tsp. (2.5 mL) sea salt

1 tsp. (5 mL) ground cinnamon

1¼ cups (310 mL) all-purpose flour

½ cup (125 mL) chopped dates

½ cup (125 mL) chopped walnuts

Japanese Cheesecake

{ MAKES ONE 8-INCH (20-CM) CAKE }

Fluffy and jiggly, Japanese cheesecake is more like a rich, flavourful sponge cake.

INGREDIENTS

1 cup (250 mL) cream cheese

¼ cup (60 mL) unsalted butter

½ cup (125 mL) whole milk

1 tbsp. (15 mL) lemon juice

1 tbsp. (15 mL) corn starch

½ cup (125 mL) cake flour

½ tsp. (2.5 mL) sea salt

6 large eggs

¾ cup (180 mL) granulated sugar

INSTRUCTIONS Preheat the oven to 300°F (150°C).

Separate the egg yolks and the egg whites into 2 different small containers.

Fill a medium saucepan with water halfway, and place on the stove over medium heat.

Position a bowl over the saucepan to create a bain marie. (see Kitchen Glossary, page 12)

Cut the cream cheese into small pieces and place in the bowl on the stove. Using a hand whisk, stir until smooth. Add the butter, milk and lemon juice. Stir well until all the ingredients are melted and are warm to the touch. Whisk in the corn starch, flour, sea salt and egg yolks until the mixture is smooth. Using the electric mixer with the whisk attachment, whip the egg whites on medium speed while gradually adding the sugar. Beat the egg whites until a light, soft meringue texture is achieved.

Remove the cream cheese mixture from the bain marie. Using a rubber spatula, gently fold the egg whites into the cream cheese mixture until fully incorporated.

Butter the inside of the springform mould. Wrap the outer sides and bottom of the cake pan in foil paper. Cut a strip of parchment paper, 1-inch (2.5-cm) higher than the springform mould and place inside the pan. Pour the cheesecake batter into the cake pan and place in a deep baking pan filled with 1-inch (2.5-cm) of water.

Bake for 35 minutes until the top of the cheesecake is light brown and has risen. Remove from oven and place on cooling rack. Chill for about 2 hours before serving.

Serve with fresh berries.

TIPS & TWISTS ....
Add 2 tbsp. (30 mL) of matcha powder or yuzu juice right before folding in the whipped egg whites.

EQUIPMENT ....
Electric mixer. Large bowl. Medium bowl. Medium saucepan. Hand whisk. Rubber spatula. 8-inch (20-cm) springform cake pan. Deep dish pan.

Chocolate & Caramel Sea Salt Popcorn Tart

{ MAKES ONE 8-INCH (20-CM) TART }

Nothing is more luscious than a silky, dark chocolate tart topped with homemade caramel sea salt popcorn. It looks stunning and tastes delicious.

INSTRUCTIONS Preheat the oven to 360°F (180°C).

Roll the chocolate dough and line an 8-in. (20-cm) round fluted tart shell. Place in the refrigerator and chill for 1 hour.

Place the chopped chocolate in a bowl.

Par bake the tart for about 20 minutes at 360°F (180°C). Remove from oven and place on a cooling rack until needed.

Pour both creams into a saucepan and bring to a boil. Remove from heat and pour over the chocolate. Let sit for a minute, then gently stir using a hand whisk until the mixture is melted—smooth and creamy.

In a small bowl, beat the egg and pour into the chocolate mixture. Stir well until the beaten egg is fully incorporated. Pour the chocolate mixture into the par-baked chocolate tart shell, then bake for just 3 minutes. Remove from the oven and place on cooling rack to cool down for 1 hour. Unmould from tart shell and place on a platter. Top with 1 cup of Caramel Sea Salt Popcorn.

TIPS & TWISTS ....
Add 1 tsp. (5 mL) of instant coffee and ½ cup (125 mL) of rum right before incorporating the beaten egg.

EQUIPMENT ....
Hand whisk. Medium saucepan. Medium bowl. Rubber spatula. 8-in. (20- cm) tart shell. Rolling pin.

INGREDIENTS

1¾ cups (430 mL) chopped dark chocolate 66%

1 cup (250. mL) whipping cream

¼ cup (60 mL) 10% cream

1 large egg

½ recipe for Extra Chocolaty Chocolate Dough found on page 20

½ recipe for Caramel Sea Salt Popcorn found on page 41

Linzer Torte

{ MAKES ONE 8-INCH (20-CM) ROUND TART }

A rich and buttery Austrian dessert, this favourite is served with a scoop of vanilla ice cream
or a simple dollop of whipped cream.

INGREDIENTS

1 cup (250 mL) ground hazelnuts

½ cup (125 mL) ground almonds

1½ (375 mL) cups all purpose flour

1 cup (250 mL) unsalted butter

⅔ cup (190 mL) granulated sugar

⅓ cup (80 mL) light brown sugar

1 tsp. (5 mL) orange zest

3 large egg yolks

½ tsp. (2.5 mL) ground cinnamon

¼ tsp. (1.25 mL) sea salt

¼ tsp. (1.25 mL) baking soda

1 large egg for egg wash

¼ cup (60 mL) icing sugar for topping

FILLING

½ recipe raspberry jam found on page 45

INSTRUCTIONS Preheat the oven to 370°F (185°C).

In an electric mixer bowl, using the paddle attachment, cream butter and both sugars on low speed until it is a light creamy texture, free of butter lumps. Add the egg yolks, one by one, scraping down the sides of the bowl each time. Add the orange zest and cinnamon.

In a medium bowl, mix by hand both ground almonds and hazelnuts, flour, sea salt and baking soda. Add the dry mix to the butter mixture and mix on low speed until the dough comes together around the paddle. Transfer the dough to a floured work surface.

Finish mixing the dough by hand and shape into a 1-inch (2.5-cm) thick rectangle brick. Wrap in plastic and refrigerate for 4 hours.

Using a rolling pin, roll out the dough to ¼-inch (.64-cm) thick, large enough to cover the entire tart shell and its sides. Shape the Linzer dough into the tart shell. Refrigerate for 10 minutes.

Roll the leftover dough into a large piece, and using a large Chef knife, cut 18 long strips—9-inches (23-cm) long and 1-inch (2.5-cm) wide. Place on a tray in the refrigerator for an hour.

Take the tart shell out of the refrigerator and fill with raspberry jam. Place 9 strips of the Linzer dough on the top, and another 9 strips on an angle to create a crisscross pattern. With a knife cut off the excess dough around the outside of the pie dish.

Beat an egg in a small bowl with a fork, and using a pastry brush, apply to the top of the pie.

Bake for 30 minutes. Rotate the pie 180 degrees and bake for another 15 minutes. Remove from the oven and place on a cooling rack. While still hot, using a small sieve, dust the top with icing sugar. Use a small knife to dislodge the sides of the pie from the mould.

TIPS & TWISTS ....
I have replaced the raspberry filling with a blueberry or apricot jam, and it is as delicious.

EQUIPMENT ....
Electric mixer. Medium bowl. Rolling pin. Rubber spatula. One 8-inch (20-cm) round 1-inch (2.5-cm) tall tart shell. Chef knife. Pastry brush.

Nori & Lemon Biscuit

{ MAKES 2 DOZEN }

*The captivating umami taste from nori makes it difficult to wait for these delectable
treats to finish baking. With a unique aroma and buttery texture, they're almost irresistible right
out of the oven. Not being a shy person about my love of eating butter, I do like to spread extra
butter on the biscuits while they're still warm from the oven.*

INSTRUCTIONS Preheat the oven to 370°F (185°C).

Using an electric mixer with the paddle attachment, combine flour,
lemon zest, sea salt, nori and baking powder on low speed. Add the diced
cold butter and continue mixing on low speed for 1 minute. Add the
cream and buttermilk and mix just enough for the dough to start to come
together. Transfer the dough to a floured work surface.

Using a rolling pin, roll out the dough to 1½-inch (3.75-cm) thick.
With a Chef knife, cut into triangles 3 x 3 x 3-inches (7.6 x 7.6 x 7.6-cm)
and place on a parchment-lined baking sheet. Brush each biscuit with
cream and sprinkle with sea salt.

Bake for 25 minutes. Remove from oven and place on a cooling rack.
Best served lukewarm.

TIPS & TWISTS ....
Add ½ cup of smoked oysters to the mixture at the same time as the
butter.

EQUIPMENT ....
Electric mixer. Pastry brush. Rolling pin. Chef knife.

INGREDIENTS

3 cups (750 mL) all
purpose flour

1 tbsp. (15 mL) lemon zest

½ cup (125 mL) granulated
sugar

½ tsp. (2.5 mL) sea salt

2 tsp. (10 mL) baking powder

1½ cups (375 mL) whipping
cream

½ cup (125 mL) buttermilk

1 cup (250 mL) diced
cold butter

¼ cup (65 mL) shredded nori

½ cup (125 mL) whipping
cream for topping

¼ cup (60 mL) sea salt flakes
for garnish

THANKS & HUGS

Sending out a heartfelt, bigger than big, huge and enormous amount of love and gratitude to the people who inspired me, helped me, coached me, trusted my heart and ideas, nurtured my soul and mind to become a better person. Without all this amazing support, there wouldn't be a cookbook.

Sergio, my son: for being the heartbeat of my life.

Fafiot, Mino and the boys: my spiritual parents and angels for the past 40 years. Thank you for showing what kindness and beauty means for all the amazing food cooked and baked with love every time we visit France.

Michele Marko & Mia Stainsby: there is never a great book without a great preface and amazing editing. Thank you both Mia and Michele.

Whitecap Books, Fitzhenry & Whiteside and Sharon Fitzhenry: thank you for your trust and support in developing my first cookbook and, I hope, many more to come.

Cecilia: for being a fantasic mother to our son Sergio.

Chef Joachim Splichal: a true mentor, the first Chef who made me understand the strength and importance of American cuisine and products. "Keep your French cooking and baking techniques but embrace what you see and feel in America," was the best advice given to me when I arrived in the U.S. 30 years ago.

Chris, Yvonne & the kiddos: for the meaning of true friendship.

Henry Wu: a trendsetter foodie, who over the course of 25 years, reshaped the Toronto food scene. When no one knew what yuzu was, we were serving it. Over the years a boss, investor, friend and, in this project, a talented photographer.

Megan Stasiewich, Ann Murray, Adrienne Panis and Rossy Earle: because no cookbook is a real cookbook without good recipe testing and styling. Thank you for all your help prepping, brainstorming, baking and tasting so many baked goods.

Anastasia Galadza: food stylist and photo shoot organizer extraordinaire.

My Family: no matter the time, no matter the distance, family is where it all started. Forever grateful to have them in my life.

The Food Group Studio, Toronto: a remarkable creative space with a "prop-alooza" of plates and utensils. It made our photo shoot so easy.

ABOUT THE CONTRIBUTORS

PHOTO BY Candace Meyer

Michelle Marko EDITOR

Michele Marko is a Vancouver-based lifestyle journalist who loves to bake and happily eats the results of her efforts. She is the former Arts & Life Editor of the *Vancouver Sun* and *Province* newspapers.

Henry M. Wu PHOTOGRAPHER

Though never his full-time profession, Henry Wu has called himself a photographer ever since daddy put a plastic, 127-format camera in his hands when he was eight years old. His original aspirations centred around photojournalism, but when the MIT-educated engineer's career took a detour into hospitality, his photographic interests made a corresponding pivot to lifestyle, architecture and food. The driving force behind more than 10 celebrated restaurants, Henry used innovative photography to explore, define and document his trendsetting collaboration with world-class celebrity chefs in the last 25 years. His editorial and marketing work appeared in national publications including *enRoute, Nuvo* and *Departures*. Now contemplating his next endeavour, Henry may be found capturing landscapes, golf architecture, and of course pretty culinary creations, in his travels.

INDEX